EXPLORING COGNITIVE DEVELOPMENT

EXPLORING COGNITIVE DEVELOPMENT: THE CHILD AS PROBLEM SOLVER

ALISON F. GARTON

Blackwell
Publishing

350 Main Street, Malden, MA 02148-5020, USA
108 Cowley Road, Oxford OX4 1JF, UK
550 Swanston Street, Carlton, Victoria 3053, Australia

First published 2004 by Blackwell Publishing Ltd

Library of Congress Cataloging-in-Publication Data

Garton, Alison, 1952-
Exploring cognitive development : the child as problem solver / Alison
F. Garton. – 1st ed.
p. cm.
Includes bibliographical references and indexes.
ISBN 0-631-23457-8 (alk. paper) – ISBN 0-631-23458-6 (pbk. : alk.
paper)
1. Problem solving in children. I. Title.
BF723.P8G37 2004
155.4′1343 – dc22

2003017215

A catalogue record for this title is available from the British Library.

Set in Rottis Serif
by SNP Best-set Typesetter Ltd., Hong Kong
Printed and bound in the United Kingdom
by MPG Books, Bodmin, Cornwall

For further information on
Blackwell Publishing, visit our website:
http://www.blackwellpublishing.com

CONTENTS

PREFACE

This book uses the example of the child as problem solver to explore theoretical issues in cognitive development.

Problem solving is taken as a microcosm for children's learning, and, specifically, collaborative problem solving is the main vehicle through which children's cognitive development can be examined. The collaborative problem solving context enables exploration of a range of contemporary theoretical perspectives that can account for children's thinking and learning.

The research that has informed this volume is large and disparate. Locally, I have benefited from the enthusiasm of students conducting research on the topic, which, to their amazement, always 'works' in so far as children demonstrate learning during the course of the experiment. Much of their work is described in this book. I have also enjoyed robust discussions on the topic with Bob Reeve at the University of Melbourne and Robin Harvey at Edith Cowan University. Thanks also to Mary Edwards for her research assistance.

This book is intended for advanced undergraduate and postgraduate students studying children's cognitive development or learning in either psychology or education programmes. It is relevant for a contemporary view of theoretical perspectives that describe and explain learning in collaborative contexts. It is not an exhaustive review but rather a selective exploration of how one paradigm can be informed by, and contribute to, a variety of explanatory theories. It is also a journey from a personal view of interaction being the key to average improvement in problem solving skills to an 'individual difference' view, taking into account the existing abilities of the child as they directly or indirectly influence the nature of the collaboration and of the learning.

Alison Garton
September 2003

CHAPTER 1

INTRODUCTION

How do children learn to think, and to use thinking or, more generally, cognition to learn? This is not a new question and, in its many guises, has challenged developmental psychologists in particular, who have sought to describe and explain the development of children's thinking. Two central questions drive cognitive development: first, what does develop in relation to children's thinking and learning, and second, how does it develop or, in other words, what mechanisms underpin the development of thinking?

Siegler (1998), in the foreword to volume 2 of the fifth edition of the *Handbook of Child Psychology*, a volume devoted to cognition, perception and language, draws attention to the plethora of approaches used to describe and explain children's cognitive development. 'Cognitive development' is generally regarded as the umbrella term under which perception, language, memory, reasoning, problem solving and learning are subsumed. Siegler also comments on areas of theorising that were new since the previous edition in 1983, including cognition as a collaborative process (Rogoff, 1998). This is important in relation to the theme of this book since, once problem solving is defined, one of the major areas of interest will be collaborative problem solving. The social aspects of problem solving in children will be highlighted, and the relationship between social development and children's thinking, learning and knowledge acquisition will be described and explained.

In contrast, another major area of theorising construes cognitive development as domain-specific. This is connected to a view that describes children's cognitive development as occurring through the operation of constraints and biases (see chapters by Wellman & Gelman, Gelman & Williams, and Woodward & Markman, 1998). So, in relation to problem solving, an alternative to the social view draws on children's innate biases in processing information or in perceiving the world, which constrain the options available during development. At least two issues emerge when discussing domain-specific knowledge or learning. First, the child is regarded as an incomplete, inadequate or incompetent version of the adult, which may not be a sustainable argument in the face of evidence from other theoretical stances. And second, the theories themselves become quite specific, rather than being broadly applicable. This swing between highly specific theories and the more general ones has characterised cognitive development research since its inception.

Siegler (1998) identifies four main trends running through the *Handbook*:

- an increased emphasis on learning – i.e., the view that what is developing leads to learning, itself an indicator of cognitive development;
- the extent and importance of variability in children's thinking and learning – i.e., taking into account individual differences between children and moving away from descriptions of the 'average' child;
- the increasing role of formal models which permit the description of mechanisms for cognitive change and development; and
- the new metaphors and units of analysis that are shaping current understanding of cognitive development.

This last trend, using metaphors to characterise children and their development, leads to varying ways of conceptualising cognitive development and hence how it is studied and the evidence required to confirm or disconfirm the metaphor. In addition, the units of analysis favoured by those studying children vary enormously – some determined by the area of interest, such as perception or language, and others by the theoretical approach being discussed or tested – and can range from the child to the parent–child dyad through to the activity itself.

A continual discussion point – and one, incidentally, about which it can be argued there is conceptual as well as terminological confusion – is the measurement of cognitive change versus cognitive development. Theoretically, this book aims to describe and explain cognitive development in children – in particular, the development of knowledge and how children learn under various conditions. However, in general, experiments with children, and, in this case, with children solving problems in dyadic interaction, demonstrate only cognitive change in one child. Such change is generally limited in scope and is sometimes dubbed 'learning'. This demonstration of cognitive change, be it short term or longer term, is taken *as evidence for* cognitive development and/or learning. While this may be regarded as 'good' science (the specific results support the theoretical position being tested, and replications, putative refutations and affirmations confirm the result), it generally does not demonstrate how learning has taken place. Not that attempts have not been made. Even the early work by Perret-Clermont and colleagues (1980) used the traditional Piagetian approach of children supporting their new-found solution with carefully reasoned and novel but consistent justifications.

Part of the debate regarding whether it is cognitive change or cognitive development that is of interest relates to the particular focus of study. Cognitive development is often studied from the individualistic perspective, looking for age-dependent trends and for ways of predicting development, with an assumption of uniformity in direction, speed of development and trajectory. Cognitive development often does not take account of different social demands and expectations placed on children, many of which vary across cultures. The mind is regarded as the font or the crucible of knowledge, and scant regard, if any, is given to the bases for the acquisition of knowledge (why does the child need to know that?) or the types of experiences that might change the nature and use of that knowledge. Cognitive development is therefore an individual progression, predictable and able to be described accurately. Cognitive change can be part of cognitive development, since age-related changes – usually improvements – in competence are measured through experimentation. But cognitive change is more amenable to a sociocultural or social influence account, since it is descriptions of individual change or learning that are being sought.

Cognitive development therefore should be regarded as the broad field within which the child as problem solver can be explored. The intention of this book is to consider the child-as-problem-solver as a microcosm through which theoretical issues in cognitive development can be examined. Some of the themes identified by Siegler (1998, 2000) will emerge, perhaps couched in slightly different ways and perhaps in a different context. This chapter identifies themes and issues that will be fleshed out in greater depth in subsequent chapters. Rather than provide a comprehensive literature review I shall discuss illustrative exemplars of research studies that consider the child as problem solver in some guise or other. The following pages provide a 'taster' of what is to come.

PROBLEM SOLVING

Problem solving can be defined as children's thinking and learning in general or as the particular tasks that children are required to solve (Garton, 1993). More specifically and more comprehensively, DeLoache, Miller and Pierroutsakos (1998) characterise problem solving as 'consist[ing] of a goal, one or more obstacles that make achieving the goal not immediately possible, one or typically more strategies that can be used to solve the problem, other resources (knowledge and other people, etc.) that can affect which strategies are used, and evaluation of the outcome of the problem-solving process' (p. 826). In this regard, DeLoache et al. can see no difference between problem solving and reasoning because each is adaptive and goal-oriented. However, the former definition (problem solving as children's thinking and learning in general) is broader and permits the inclusion of specific content areas such as language to be a problem requiring a solution in its own right. Nonetheless it would be possible, if it were considered desirable, to specify, for example, goals, obstacles, strategies and other resources that facilitate the child's acquisition of language or of number. So the broad and specific definitions proffered so far are not incompatible. Is there, therefore, any distinction between problem solving and reasoning? I would argue that – based on the comments above and the definition to be used in this book and given that problem solving can refer to both the activity *and* the task – then yes, it can be distinguished from reasoning, which normally refers solely to the cognitive activity, or the particular task a child is required to solve.

In relation to the study of children as problem solvers, problems are regarded as cognitive tasks that require solutions. They are typically characterised by a discrepancy between the present state or current situation and the desired state, solution or goal. Whether or not a problem exists depends on the expertise and knowledge of the person (adult or child) perceiving there to be such a discrepancy. In the case of children's development, adults, who may be parents or curious developmental psychology researchers, will usually identify the problem solving task, be it language *per se*, a jigsaw puzzle, or understanding the storyline in *Teletubbies*, taking into account the child's age, current level of learning and development (either via personal knowledge or through pre-testing) and the particular domain under investigation. So, parents will decide whether an activity is to be defined as a 'problem' for their child, and will use their knowledge of their child's capabilities in that domain to extend or to constrain the child's knowledge and skills. It is often claimed that this requires sensitivity on the part of parents, though accounts of how this sensitivity is 'acquired' or 'develops' are nonexistent. Experimental psychologists base their assignment of the label 'problem' to a child's activity or task on their theoretical knowledge, as well as through pre-testing children on similar tasks or testing similar abilities. A perceived discrepancy between current knowledge and skills and potential knowledge and skills can, in both cases, lead to problem solving, usually best described as learning.

Regarding problem solving as closer to learning than to reasoning enables a broader conceptualisation of what can sometimes be defined rather narrowly. That does not mean that some of the characteristics of problem solving described by DeLoache et al. (1998) are not applicable. They are, and it is useful to reiterate them here:

> Children's problem solving is marked by flexibility and opportunism from an early age, but their performances are limited by the strategies they have access to, the resources available for problem solving, their ability to manage the process of solving problems, and the social contexts in which problems are presented and vanquished. (p. 826)

With the exception of the word 'vanquished', which conveys an unfortunate sense of finality, this sentence encapsulates what I hope to 'unpack' in this book. However, this will be done by using problem solving to explore strategies, resources, activities and social contexts that support and facilitate children's learning, cognitive development and knowledge acquisition.

Collaborative problem solving is problem solving that involves more than the individual child. Instead of focusing exclusively on the individual child to describe and explain developmental changes in cognition, learning and knowledge, there is a shift to the dyad, to the group (however defined, up to and including the social–historical–cultural context) and to the activity, the problem itself. It is also important to distinguish peer collaboration from things such as peer tutoring and reciprocal teaching. Although the latter two are considered types of collaborative learning (e.g., King, 2002; Palincsar & Herrenkohl, 2002), in peer tutoring there is a more competent or knowledgeable child who is expected to teach a novice or less knowledgeable child. There is no sense of equality of roles and responsibilities, of co-operation or of mutuality, as it describes a unidirectional process. Reciprocal teaching involves co-operation among peers together with instruction, usually provided by an adult teacher: It is a classroom teaching strategy. The teacher scaffolds the peers' efforts at learning while providing some direct instruction, thus tacitly supporting the co-operative learning of the children. Collaborative problem solving, as construed in this book, refers to the joint efforts of pairs – some of which may indeed have intentionally divergent competencies, though often not given a designated role as novice or expert – to work towards a mutual understanding of or solution to a single problem.

Considering problem solving as collaboration enables a shift away from describing children's cognitive development in terms of what is 'average' or expected for children of a particular age, preferably universally, to a consideration of the child in a social context and all that this entails. Viewing children as individuals within a social context allows us as researchers to adopt an individualistic approach to cognitive development, whereby ultimately children's learning profiles can be charted and used to make between-children comparisons and between-age comparisons. Profiles allow for developmental patterns to be identified and for children's cognitive development to be considered in both broad and specific contexts.

From time to time, I prefer to use the term 'social interaction', a more generic phrase than 'collaborative problem solving' and sometimes a more accurate descriptor for the facilitatory process when more than one person is involved. In addition, it is assumed that during social interaction or collaborative problem solving, the participant with the lesser knowledge benefits, and this is manifested in enhanced learning or greater knowledge. It is typically argued then that the interaction or the collaboration has had a beneficial or facilitatory effect on the child's cognitive development. While this assumption is derived from social–historical–cultural explanations of cognitive development, it is not necessarily incompatible with theoretical explanations that focus on innate constraints or biases, or on approaches that consider problem solving failure as well as success as a catalyst for cognitive change, learning and knowledge acquisition.

SOCIAL EXPLANATIONS FOR COGNITIVE CHANGE

Social explanations for cognitive change have taken many forms. The major social explanatory theories are summarised below, with greater detail being provided in subsequent chapters.

Piaget described children's cognitive change during interaction as a consequence of *cognitive conflict*, although he was essentially concerned with the development of mental operations, conceptualised as internalised coordinations of actions. These operations allowed greater flexibility in thinking as children got older. Children's thinking progressed from being sensory–motor, through pre-operational thought, to fully operational thought whereby abstract mental operations, such as reversibility (the ability to understand that an inverse action can cause the original physical or mental state to be regained), can be used on a range of materials. Cognitive development was characterised as qualitative changes in thinking, changes that occurred as result of adaptation of existing cognitive structures. The child was considered to be an active constructor of his or her knowledge. Change was inevitable and irreversible, determined biologically, although the time required for change may vary from individual to individual, influenced by different levels of environmental stimulation. Piaget believed that the environment played little role in the direction of the changes, only in their duration; it could provide general direction, not specific experiences, to influence cognitive change.

When it was discussed, social interaction, specifically between peers, was postulated by Piaget (1932) as having a facilitatory effect on children's developing understanding of morality. Piaget was interested in how children came to solutions to moral dilemmas rather than the solutions *per se*. In the discussions generated by questioning them about moral dilemmas, children demonstrated a shift from an amoral stance when younger than age seven, where behaviour was regulated by others, to an awareness of moral rules. These rules are firstly external to the child but eventually are internalised as an awareness of their reciprocal nature. In order to achieve 'autonomous morality', Piaget proposed that peer interaction provides the necessary experience of different points of view, which leads to children thinking about moral rules and developing their own system of justice. In particular, co-operation and fairness in social relations are emphasised.

If conflict was regarded as the major mechanism for cognitive development according to Piagetian and post-Piagetian theory (e.g., Doise, 1978; Perret-Clermont, 1980), then *collaboration* would be a better characterisation of the mechanism for cognitive change proposed by Vygotsky. Vygotsky's theory of development (best discussed for our purposes in his 1978 translation) assumes that cognitive development does not occur in isolation. It co-occurs with language development, social development and even physical development, and these developments occur in a social and cultural context. This holistic approach focuses attention on the importance of taking into account all facets of an individual's development, including the broader social, historical, cultural, even economic factors that contribute to an individual's cognitive competence. In addition to regarding the child's development in its social and cultural context, Vygotsky's theory claims that cognitive and language development are explicable and comprehensible only by reference to these contexts. That is, the processes of cognitive growth depend on and acknowledge social contexts and influences.

The central mechanism for learning is the transfer of responsibility for the achievement of a mutually acceptable goal or solution from an expert, or more adept participant, to a novice, or naive participant, in collaborative interaction. The responsibility entails planning and monitoring the strategies for accomplishing success, operationalising the most expedient, efficient and effective strategies, and demonstrating mastery of all aspects of the task. In so doing, success – i.e. attainment of the desired goal – is also usually achieved.

To this end, Vygotsky postulated the existence of the *zone of proximal development* (ZPD). This is defined as the distance between the child's actual developmental level and his or her potential developmental level, as seen when the child is solving problems in interaction with 'an adult or more capable peer' (Vygotsky, 1978, p. 86). The ZPD is a measure of learning potential and represents the region wherein cognitive development takes place. It implies a degree of collaboration between participants in the social interaction, where each is making a contribution towards the goal. These participants may come from different starting points and may not agree on the definition of the problem or the means to solve it.

Part of the task of the ZPD is to permit intersubjectivity and task definition. *Intersubjectivity* occurs when the two participants share the same task, or situation definition, and each knows the other shares the same definition. It can be defined as a 'meeting of minds'. Thus, not only is the child guided and supported to accomplish the solution, but he or she also learns how to achieve mutuality and intersubjectivity, both instrumental to task success.

The achievement of intersubjectivity depends partly on the contributions made by each participant in the interaction. Demarcation of roles facilitates learning, possibly for both participants. The novice, or less competent participant, determines the existing level of skill or expertise and sets the pace for instruction and learning. The more experienced participant gauges the pre-existing skills and the necessity for instruction, and divides the task or problem into manageable components. The adult or more capable peer takes responsibility for the management of the task and also for changing the definition of the task by the child or the less capable peer.

It is useful to differentiate the ZPD from the notion of *scaffolding* proposed by Bruner and colleagues (see Wood, Bruner & Ross, 1976). Scaffolding refers to the process of adult support and assistance given to a child mastering a locally determined problem. The problem may be a cognitive one or may be language *per se*, and scaffolding refers to the sensitivity of a parent to the child's potential. The ZPD is a theoretical construct that describes that potential, the distance between unaided and aided competence. Scaffolding refers to the aid component, with emphasis on the provision of appropriate support for successful learning. Gauvain (2001b) describes chronologically how scaffolding, or contingent responding, on the part of the parent (usually the mother) changes as children develop and master different tasks and solve different problems. She concludes:

Children are involved with more experienced partners for a very large portion of their daily lives, and these experiences often involve solving problems. . . . during these interactions adults assist children in the development and use of many of the skills critical for solving problems . . . research does suggest that social interaction with adults is an important source of input for children during the years in which they are developing and refining their problem solving skills. (Gauvain, 2001b, p. 155)

CHANGE IN THE CONTEXT OF INTERACTIVE/COLLABORATIVE PROBLEM SOLVING

Instead of looking at aspects of the problem solving situation to find explanations of cognitive change during interaction, an alterative approach is to look at aspects of the child. Given that improvement is noted in the less capable child during and after interactive problem solving, how can this happen at the level of the child him or herself? In looking at the individual child in the social context, the question can then be posed: What does the child bring to the task? As noted previously, Vygotsky acknowledged that children or participants in collaborative problem solving may begin from different starting points. Thus, we can look at the existing level, ability or capacity of each child – in other words, their competencies on entry to the task. Alternatively, or in addition, we can look at the propensity or potential to change in each child in the problem solving interaction.

Bonino and Cattelino (1999), for example, examined the relationship between cognitive and social abilities in children, specifically looking at the relationship between flexibility in thinking and the solution to social conflicts with peers. For the purposes of their research study, flexibility was defined as 'reactive flexibility', which requires children to shift their responses in relation to external cues. In this case, the researchers used the Wisconsin Card Sorting Task, a categorisation task requiring the inhibition of responses that have been rewarded in order to attain a new classification. This was chosen because the peer task required the children to shift their actions in responses to the demands of the task and of their partners.

Underpinning this study then was the notion that flexibility would influence interaction behaviours such as competition and co-operation, and the achievement of a solution or goal. The specific hypothesis was that children with higher flexibility in thinking as measured at pre-test would be more co-operative and less competitive in social conflicts. Lower flexibility children, on the other hand, would demonstrate more aggression and less co-operation. Using seven-year-old children, this study supported the hypothesis, but more generally showed that a pre-existing disposition on the part of the children – in this case a level of cognitive flexibility – influenced the nature of the interaction between pairs of children.

Furthermore, interpersonal capacities that may enhance the facilitative nature of collaborative problem solving can be explored and measured. For example, Da Silva and Winnykamen (1998) examined the role of personal attributes in subsequent problem solving success. Children's sociability levels were measured, based on peer nomination and rating, and children were paired with another similar-aged child on the basis of performance on a problem solving task. Specific hypotheses about the outcomes for different dyads were constructed. For the six-year-old children in this study, sociability was found to influence individual pre- to post-test learning, although gains were recorded for lower ability children who worked with higher ability peers as well as children who worked with same ability peers. Sociable children, as predicted, demonstrated better levels of communication as well as co-operative behaviours that were adapted to their partner's needs and to the exchange of information. In general, it was concluded that sociable children were sensitive to their partner during interaction and this facilitated subsequent learning.

DOMAIN SPECIFIC KNOWLEDGE

A way of conceptualising children's increasing ability to solve problems is by viewing cognitive development within specifiable domains of knowledge, including language, number, psychology and biology. Certain cognitive processes, such as analogy, basic perceptual or cognitive processes, or category representation, which are domain-independent, can be regarded as constraining the more general sociocultural mechanisms of development. That is, the more general explanations of children's problem solving can only be interpreted within the context of domain-specific knowledge. In this way, cognitive development can be explained by describing the constraints that operate to affect the growth of understanding within specifiable domains of knowledge. This does not mean, however, that sociocultural explanations are ignored; indeed they can be accommodated within such explanations that take into account not only the domain of knowledge but also the culture or semiotics of meaning.

A consequence of taking a domain-specific view is that the nature of the 'problem' under investigation becomes important. Furthermore, such a focus permits the specification of the nature of knowledge and any changes in that knowledge that may occur as a function of, for example, collaboration. Consequently, cognitive growth, change and development can be specified quite precisely, in contrast to the general changes described when invoking more global explanations of cognitive change. From this perspective, it has been argued that the mechanisms for change on subsequent improved problem solving have thus largely been uninterpretable because:

- entry competence is unknown;
- the developmental sequence is unknown;
- the theoretical consequences of change are not usually articulated; and
- perhaps most importantly, the nature of the qualitative or quantitative change is unknown.

CHILDREN'S POTENTIAL TO CHANGE

In order to examine children's potential to change, it is helpful to redefine cognitive change as knowledge acquisition. Furthermore, the literature on knowledge acquisition that has used a problem solving context has focused specifically on children's strategy development and deployment. In other words, the literature on children's strategy use has tended to focus on knowledge acquisition *per se*, rather than cognitive changes, although this may represent only a change of emphasis or of terminology.

The underlying assumption of research that has looked at change in children's thinking or strategy use is that children have multiple ways of thinking about any one problem. Even from the early days of Piagetian-inspired research, it has been recognised that children can demonstrate different ways of thinking or use different strategies, depending on the context. What more recent research has been examining is how these multiple ways of thinking arise and how children choose between them.

In examining the context in which cognitive change/knowledge acquisition takes place, Kuhn, Garcia-Mila, Zohar and Andersen (1995) ask the question, 'How much freedom do children have in selecting the evidence on which to base their solution to a problem?' In the experimental tasks typically used to study children's problem solving, the answer is 'Not a lot'. By constraining the options available to the children via defining or selecting the problem for them, their strategy selection and use can be studied within the parameters we, as adult experimenters, think are important. Methodologically, Kuhn et al. claim to have overcome this difficulty through the use of a multiple-task, multiple-occasion assessment of children's strategy use. However, more generally, the question is one of how existing knowledge constrains current strategy deployment as well as the acquisition of new knowledge. As an extension of this, a further question is then how and when does new evidence, construed as success or failure on a new task, lead to changes in thinking? What constitutes 'new evidence'? Kuhn et al. argue that change arises slowly, with old strategies not simply replaced with new ones; instead they all compete for use and application, depending on the problem and the context. What does change is a distribution of use of a set of strategies, each of varying adequacy for the particular problem. Transfer is not a simple single operation, but rather requires domain-specific knowledge such as analogy or representation.

Siegler and colleagues have explored in greater depth the notion of how children choose between different strategies, and in so doing they have developed a model of strategy choice – the Adaptive Strategy Choice Model (ASCM) (Siegler, 1996). In developing the ASCM, metacognitive models, as postulated by Kuhn et al. as well as by Flavell (e.g., 1999), are dismissed as inadequate. Although metacognitive models are rationally derived and pay attention to explicit and conscious knowledge about one's own cognition and cognitive processes, Siegler believes their greatest value has been in informing more recent research on children's developing awareness and understanding of themselves and others. So while they have not contributed to greater knowledge about how children choose between alternative strategies when faced with a problem, metacognitive models have led on to studies of children's theories of mind. Siegler meanwhile demonstrated that children typically think in multiple ways about a problem and that there is great variability and multidimensionality in the ways children think in general.

Karmiloff-Smith's (1992) theory of development relies on representational change being 'success-driven', while behavioural change is more often 'failure-driven'. Three recurrent phases of strategy change are noted in all domains where problems, broadly construed, are encountered and solved. In the first, procedural, phase, every problem is regarded separately from any other and solutions are data-driven. Success is the goal, and children lack an overall integrative strategy for solving problems. Increasing automaticity is generated only by increasing success. The second, metaprocedural, phase involves the rewriting of the earlier individual procedures as representations, and problems are solved according to the appropriate representation. This paradoxically often results in children apparently not achieving successful solutions to problems as they focus on deployment of the strategy represented. The final, conceptual, phase is marked by greater flexibility in the use of problem solving strategies, spurred on by success rather than failure to achieve the correct solution.

The model proposed by Karmiloff-Smith generalises to all problem solving domains, including language, mathematics, drawing and music.

THEORIES OF MIND

A possible mechanism to draw together the research on communication and awareness of the other in interaction and the choice of strategies in problem solving is the child's developing theories of mind. Strategy choice may be a result of conscious awareness and reflection of the content of thought (Kuhn et al., 1995), although Siegler (1996) argues that it is not. (Indeed, Siegler goes as far as arguing that strategy choice is based on 'mindless' processes.) Pursuing the line of argument put forward by Kuhn and colleagues, if both participants in a collaborative problem solving situation share a common conception of the problem and how to solve it, then the degree to which they can work successfully on the task is enhanced. Such a shared task perspective can be achieved by talking to one another. Similarly, explicit or implicit conflict between children can be resolved through communication. Social regulation via communication about role division and allocation, as well as planning and executing the task, facilitates problem solving and can be beneficial to both participants (Garton, 1992, 1993; Teasley, 1995).

A theoretical explanation comes from a large body of recent research that has demonstrated the importance for children of being able to reflect on knowledge. The development of children's 'theory of mind' is concerned with developing understanding of the nature of knowledge and refers to the ability of children to understand that others too know things, have beliefs and can think, based on knowledge which might be true or false. One crucial means to such understanding is through communication as evidenced in collaborative problem solving. However, it may be that communication can only be successful if there is an existing propensity, or awareness, in children to recognise the importance of the strategic knowledge of the other partner in the interaction.

Chapman (1991) proposes the epistemic triangle to permit inclusion of social interaction in children's reasoning on concrete operational tasks. This construct integrates a Piagetian view, which focuses on the role of the developing child interacting with the environment, and a Vygotskian view, which places social interaction in the forefront. In the epistemic triangle, there is recognition of both the object in the environment and the communicative and social nature of the human interaction. The development of social understanding takes place alongside the child's construction of knowledge of the physical world. This view has been extended by

Carpendale and Lewis (in press) to account for the child's developing understanding of the mind. According to these researchers, children construct an understanding of how they and others acquire knowledge through communication in interaction.

THE WAY FORWARD

As explained earlier, my aim is to explore how the child as problem solver can be used as a microscope with which to discuss contemporary issues in theoretical approaches to cognitive development. In particular, I wish to regard the child in a social context and not as a solitary, even lonely, individual. It has always been my belief that children require social support to learn, and the problem solving situation is undoubtedly social. It is all the more interesting if we regard it as collaborative, in so far as there is a requirement that children, or children and adults, work together, create a social context and share roles and responsibilities to achieve an outcome or to solve a problem. Not all the theories to be discussed evolve from collaborative problem solving. Instead, the research presented has used a problem solving paradigm in some shape or form to discuss various aspects of the participants, the task or the context within a particular theoretical framework. Thus we have theories that look at how the nature and type of interaction influences the outcome, theories that look at characteristics of the participants such as their gender or their capacity to generate strategies or solutions, and theories that claim all learning is innate. With these in mind, my exploration begins.

CHAPTER 2

THEORETICAL OVERVIEW

There are many theories that have been used to describe and explain children's cognitive development, some of them applicable across a range of domains, others having more limited explanatory power. Valsiner (1998) draws attention to the 'increasing fragmentation' (p. 190) of our knowledge in developmental psychology, related in part to the use of the inductive approach and its reliance on the 'scientific method' and statistical analyses. The methodologies as applied to children of various ages, capabilities or ethnicities have led to the proliferation of theories, principles and speculations about the nature of development in one or a number of domains. Valsiner believes the focus on methodology has been at the cost of a theoretical focus on development *per se*.

Valsiner (1998) sets out three constraints in our ability to maintain a consistent theoretical perspective in developmental psychology:

1. the irreversible nature of development;
2. the complexity of the developing structure (be it the individual, the social group or whatever); and
3. the complexity of the environment in which it is developing (Bronfenbrenner, 1979) and the multiple levels of the developing structure and of the environment.

Although this book is concerned with the study of children's problem solving, this should be regarded as illustrative for the purposes of examining some of these empirical and theoretical issues. In the case of problem solving, interest lies in how development, characterised as learning, occurs, and how various factors both within the child and in the environment, characterised as social interaction, influence the cognitive development of children. It is necessary to restrict the focus simply because it is not possible to make detailed observations of all of children's development, precisely because of the complexities discussed by Valsiner.

As noted in Chapter 1, where each was introduced and briefly described, two major theorists, Piaget and Vygotsky, dominate the various theoretical positions that exist in developmental psychology. Each is best known for the breadth and depth of his theory as well as its extensive and enduring influence, and each has made a contribution in relation to collaborative problem solving, much of it already reviewed (see, for example, Garton, 1992; Thornton, 1995; Tudge & Rogoff, 1989). Piaget's model is sometimes regarded as an equilibration model and aligned more closely with biology and philosophy than mainstream psychology (Valsiner, 1998). In Piaget's constructionist model, equilibration is a dynamic state resulting from a balance between assimilation, the process whereby new experiences are incorporated into existing schemes or mental representations, and accommodation, the process by which new representations are modified based on experience (Garton, 2003). Vygotsky's theory has been placed by Valsiner (1998) alongside models of teaching and learning, models that include at least one person in addition to the developing child. In Chapter 1 each of the theories was briefly described and discussed as a social explanatory theory. This clearly places the emphasis for the cognitive change noted after social interaction on the process of the interaction itself, while acknowledging the skills the children bring to the interaction which may influence and be influenced by the interaction itself. So although Vygotsky's theory is often regarded as an antidote to Piaget's theory through its recognition of the necessity of another person for development, this is not strictly the case. I have taken this as the starting point for my discussion and comparison of the theories of Piaget and Vygotsky.

While both Piaget and Vygotsky regarded the social environment as providing some of the necessary impetus for cognitive change, the means or processes by which this was postulated as happening were not the same. In addition, the actual form of the social environment varied in subtle yet important ways. Much of the illustrative work conducted and cited by Piaget (and subsequent authors who used the Piagetian explanatory framework, such as Doise & Mugny, 1984; Kruger, 1992, 1993; Perret-Clermont, 1980) has examined peer interaction. Peer interaction includes dyads or larger groupings of, typically, same gender, same age and/or same ability children. These children jointly construct a single representation of knowledge, through the resolution of initially different perspectives to one common view. Vygotsky's observations and experiments by contrast emphasise the nature of process in a teaching/learning co-constructive environment, which by definition requires a teacher, usually an adult or more capable peer, and a learner. In both cases, the nature of the 'problem' under investigation, and hence needing to be solved, also varies, and this too must be taken into account. This will be discussed in greater depth later in this chapter, alongside the issue of just which tasks are suitable vehicles for the study of children's problem solving, depending on the theoretical position being tested or explored. These areas of difference are important for consideration of the role of the social world in promoting, facilitating and benefiting children's cognitive development.

Siegler (1996) discusses limitations of current theories of cognitive development, drawing attention to the problems associated with accounts of the mechanisms of development. He acknowledges that most developmentalists are eclectic, a trait shared with many other sorts of psychologists, particularly clinicians who do not want to be associated with any particular approach and see themselves as somehow more broad-minded. This book perhaps demonstrates such eclecticism in so far as one single paradigm, children's problem solving, can be explained by many theories and has itself been used to exemplify or study all sorts of phenomena. The major complaint as far as developmental psychologists are concerned is the plethora of descriptions of age-related averages in the absence of explanations of change. Some of the debate arises from confusion, much of which can be traced simply to terminology and careless use of words such as 'change', 'learning' and 'development', as discussed in Chapter 1, although the words have applicability to the object of investigation and the way it is studied.

Lerner (1998) deals with the distinction between cognitive change and cognitive development at a high level of abstraction when he opens his review chapter with a reflection on the comments made by Mussen in 1970. Mussen noted that developmental theory has largely been confined to explanations of psychological change, and change in psychological processes rather than in structures or functions. There is no reason to dispute these prescient comments. As Lerner notes, contemporary views of psychological development are more or less restricted to 'conceptions of process' (p. 1) and are not tied to a particular domain. Again, this present volume will use a particular domain – problem solving – as an example to highlight the processes depicted in various explanations of children's cognitive change.

PIAGET AND VYGOTSKY: IS THERE ANY COMMON GROUND?

In more recent times, instead of proposing the theories of Vygotsky and Piaget as alternative and opposing explanations of the role and function of collaborative problem solving in cognitive development, commentators have been seeking to find common ground and themes in the theories. I will be considering the relevance of these commonalities, if any, for the study of collaborative problem solving. The debates have tended to focus on broader epistemological and ontological issues, and it is important to explore what these debates mean for the role of the 'social', its definition in children's collaborative solving and ultimately for the explanation of cognitive development.

In somewhat simplistic terms, Piaget's theory is often characterised as an 'inside-out' one, while Vygotsky's is regarded as an 'outside-in' theory. This means that Piaget generally construed the child's cognition as developing independently of any environmental or social influence. The direction of development is genetically predetermined, and the child has to construct knowledge him or herself. The speed at which this happens depends on various internal and external factors; the direction is specified in advance. Vygotsky, on the other hand, regarded cognitive development as reflecting the child's social, historical and cultural background. Children's developing knowledge is a product of the particular social context in which they find themselves. In addition, particular expert support and guidance 'lend a hand' during teaching to benefit the novice child as he or she learns.

However, with deeper analysis, it is not obvious that the two theorists had such divergent views. Wozniak (1996) drew together a number of areas where Piaget and Vygotsky apparently demonstrated convergence in their considerations of some aspects of the social environment. Despite Piaget's apparent neglect of the social world, Wozniak finds that both he and Vygotsky emphasised interaction, defined as 'mind as an active, organising principle, collaborating with the environment in transforming thought towards an increasingly delicate adaptation of thought to things and things to thought' (p. 14). This description allows for inclusion of the Piagetian principle of assimilation and the Vygotskian principle of environmental relativity, whereby, to be effective, the environment should be conducive to the child's level of development. In this way, a common definition of interaction, implying a social component, can be found.

Secondly, the dialectical conceptions of development espoused by each theorist were similar in so far as each described development as occurring through oppositions that are then transcended to permit transformation and integration of structure. In other words, they each believed in the separation of structure from function, and, for both Piaget and Vygotsky, structural organisation required the integration of lower structural levels into higher ones. Development was thus described as systemic and hierarchical. Again, this represents another area of commonality.

Finally, Wozniak (1996) points out that both Piaget and Vygotsky used a clinical method to obtain the observations that enabled them to build their theories. In particular, each used a qualitative technique that fostered the co-construction of knowledge between the experimenter and the participant. This is quite a different methodology from that commonly accepted as permitting the objectivity required by science to construct a theory. Indeed, one of the major early criticisms of Piaget's theory was its lack of methodological rigour, and much work in the 1960s and 1970s was undertaken to demonstrate the scientific merit or otherwise of Piaget's experimental methods and hence the theory. (For an excellent summary of an alternative, see Donaldson, 1978.)

Despite these three 'converging homologies', Wozniak (1996, p. 14) also highlights some areas of divergence. The two major ones he believes derive exclusively from Vygotsky's socio-historico-cultural theoretical view, which emphasised the role of society and history in the transformation of the child's developing mind. According to this view, children's knowledge develops, or is transformed, through acculturation into a particular system of meanings by which individuals make sense of their experience. These meanings are actively constructed, and reflect, or are an acculturated outcome of, the society in which the child is developing. While Vygotsky's untimely death did not permit full development and elaboration of his theory, its strength lies in its power to explain all sorts of areas of development, including cognition, language and perception, as well as specific areas such as semantic development, reading and problem solving.

However, according to Wozniak, two fundamental criticisms that can be levelled at Vygotsky's theory are, firstly, that it fails to address normative development: that is, it does not answer questions about what development is and how it can take place. So, for example, it is impossible to distinguish between the knowledge of a child and the knowledge of an adult, in a developmental sense. Change can be described but it seems that development cannot. Secondly, the theory apparently overstates the discontinuity between biological (primary) and social (secondary) systems of function: that is, the theory distinguishes between the primitive mind and practical intelligence of the child and the acculturated mind and reflective intelligence of the adult.

In making these criticisms, Wozniak draws on Piaget's theory to show how his different views further highlight these weaknesses. In relation to the normative criteria for development, two approaches can be taken to the problem of demonstrating how the mind of the adult is more developed than the mind of the child. In Piaget's universalist view, development can be described through the specification of domain-specific criteria. The mechanism of equilibration was specified as the domain-independent criterion of development, and thus development was viewed as the change in lower levels that leads to equilibrium in higher level cognitive structures.

An alternative view, an historical approach, and largely consistent with Vygotsky's theory, is that development unfolds according to a temporal sequence. In a pattern reminiscent of ontogeny recapitulating phylogeny, higher evolutionary development (including human chronological development) is assumed to be superior to lower evolutionary development. Psychological development in adults is regarded as more advanced than the primitive intelligence of the child (or the ape). In arguing that this position is problematic, apart from the sociopolitical flavour, Wozniak (1996) points out that this view does not allow for regression, and Vygotsky himself did not develop a theoretical position that argues for or against the possibility of regression. The other argument against the historical approach lies in its simplistic cross-species and cross-historical comparisons and their relevance to developmental psychology.

In relation to continuity/discontinuity between action or practical intelligence and thought or reflective intelligence, it is argued that Piaget's theory supported a continuity view whereby thought is intimately derived from action (particularly in the sensory-motor period). Vygotsky again, largely because his theory was incomplete, was 'ambivalent' (Wozniak, 1996, p. 19), although he seems to have explicated a view whereby internalisation of tool use may characterise development. This could appear either to contradict or to support a discontinuity view, depending on how you view the process.

It is useful to reflect on the differences or similarities between the theories of Piaget and Vygotsky. For the purposes of discussing children's collaborative problem solving, it is encouraging to note the level of interest shown by contemporary developmental and educational psychologists in delineating the commonalities, especially in relation to the theoretical relevance of the social environment for cognitive development. Indeed, it is the earlier simplification of the difference between the two theorists that has led to the search for the social in Piaget's theory and the concomitant resultant comparison with Vygotsky's theory.

In an edited book, Tryphon and Vonèche (1996) include a number of chapters by eminent psychologists who explore the relationship between Piaget and Vygotsky, in particular their relative influences on one another, given they were contemporaries, both born in 1896. One of the major puzzles that continues to be debated is the extent to which Piaget and Vygotsky exchanged views and the circumstances that prevented any meaningful dialogue between them. While one can speculate as to why Piaget never responded to comments Vygotsky made in relation to Piaget's view of egocentric speech (now incorporated as Chapter 2 in *Thought and*

Language, 1986), history cannot be reversed, so it will forever remain a mystery. This, compounded by Vygotsky's early demise, meant that the two never engaged in dialogue or debate, although they would have been aware of each other's work. They certainly never met. It has been left to more recent discussion among experts to explore similarities and differences in their philosophies, ideologies, aims and approaches. A plethora of work was published in 1996, the centenary of the birth of each theorist (e.g., Tryphon & Vonèche, 1996; *Human Development* (1996), Vol 31, Special Issue), although work comparing the two at various depths of debate has appeared in the psychological literature since the 1980s. (For an earlier volume where comparisons are touched on, see Wertsch, 1985, and for a review up to the early 1990s, see Garton, 1992.)

Rogoff (1998) discusses the compatibility of the theories of Piaget and Vygotsky. Obviously there are places where there is divergence (as has been noted), but there is sufficient commonality to enable a useful comparison to be made, particularly in relation to their views on cognition as a collaborative process (the title of Rogoff's chapter). The key commonality is their emphasis on the achievement of shared thinking through collaboration. When they work together to solve a problem, children build on a common ground that is not necessarily shared, since each has a unique perspective. A shared focus of attention allows for the establishment of common ground through a process of mutual agreement or intersubjectivity. Intersubjectivity, the co-construction of a common representation of the problem, is achieved through communication between people (Garton, 1992, 1993; Rogoff, 1998). In achieving this mutuality, each participant in the collaborative process must modify his or her perspective in order to understand the perspective of the other, and these changes form the basis of cognitive development as well as cognitive change as measured through performance on the problem solving task. Support for the role of shared thinking through communication can be found in each theoretical position, even if the manifestation is different. For Piaget, conflict and disagreement characterised the establishment of shared understanding, while for Vygotsky, it was achieved through co-operation and collaboration, largely in the ZPD.

Rogoff (1998) provides a helpful historical perspective on the development of the views of both Piaget and Vygotsky. In addition to covering the origins and tenets of Vygotsky's theory, Rogoff notes that instead of focusing on the individual in human development, Vygotsky proposed a method of analysis into units that have all the basic characteristics of the whole and offer a dynamic system of meaning (Vygotsky, 1986). This use of a unit that incorporates the functions of the larger system, including the social, the historical and the cultural, has been influential for modern-day theorists who have debated and adopted various units of analysis. Their main defining characteristic, however, is that they maintain and reflect the larger systemic functions. Current sociocultural approaches and theories (e.g., Shweder, Goodnow, Hatano, Levine, Markus & Miller, 1998) maintain this general tradition, as does the dynamic systems approach to change (e.g., Thelen & Smith, 1994).

In relation to Piaget's theory, Rogoff (1998) reminds us that in his early work he discussed the role of co-operation in resolving cognitive conflicts that arose from different perspectives. As mentioned previously, this work was continued through Piaget's discussion of the child's moral development. However, Piaget restricted the social world to simply the interpersonal; there was no consideration given to the broader social (or cultural) context in which the child was growing up. For Piaget, growth and development took place on the individual level. By contrast, Vygotsky regarded development and learning as intertwined, a product of the immediate and broader social environment, co-constructed by the participants at a particular place and time. This gives rise to an important distinction between the theories of Vygotsky and Piaget: for Piaget, individuals work *independently* on the ideas and actions of one another, while for Vygotsky, individuals work in collaboration and partnership *together* and *jointly*. This fundamental difference between the definition of what constitutes the social world and how it 'works' has implications for the study and interpretation of research on collaborative problem solving in children. In particular, the locus of change (Rogoff, 1998, p. 684), either the individual or the interaction, varies. According to Rogoff, in a Piagetian framework, co-operation between children can lead to equilibrium in individual children through processes such as communication, reciprocity and recognition of contradiction. It is also claimed that Piaget believed social interaction would not be beneficial for children until middle childhood, after egocentricity has been overcome with the development of concrete operations. Egocentricity blocks reciprocity and the ability to entertain other points of view. Genuine exchange of ideas between children is not possible until they can recognise alternative points of view, maintain and alter their own perspective as necessary, and argue and justify the rationale.

Furthermore, social interaction is regarded as an opportunity for children with different opinions, perspectives and views to engage in discussion, to exchange those views and to seek alternatives. Unlike the Vygotskian view where the interaction itself enables the construction of shared thinking, the Piagetian framework regards the children's views as independent. These views are then shared in social interaction and comparisons made of the information. This is not the same as co-constructed collaboration where a single view or position derives from the intersubjectivity created by the interaction. Thus the two theoretical positions offer quite different ways of regarding the role and function of social interaction. It can also be claimed that cognitive change resulting from cognitive conflict results in cognitive development, since Piagetian theory can explain and predict cognitive change. Alternatively, cognitive change resulting from intersubjectivity and collaboration is a manifestation of learning and not of cognitive development at all.

Rogoff (1998) comments that Piagetian theory has, however, 'added new ideas' (p. 686) to sociocultural theory. The study of the role of cognitive conflict between peers has led to the consideration of the social context within which cognitive development occurs. The argument is that children paired with similar status peers can benefit *because of* the equality of the relationship, as this facilitates the adoption of alternative perspectives. It is easier to listen to your peers than to take account of the views of experts or adults.

PEER INTERACTION: VARIOUS PERSPECTIVES

An illustrative example of research that has tested the Piagetian hypothesis that cognitive conflict is responsible for cognitive change is that reported by Kruger and colleagues. Kruger also attempts to place her results in a Vygotskian framework, allowing a direct comparison of the theoretical positions using the same experimental design and data (although some of the data were re-analysed post hoc). In arguing for the facilitatory effect of conflicting perspectives from peers, Kruger (1992, 1993) considers the distinction between conflict and co-operation in peer collaboration. She examines transactive discussions both between children and their same-aged peers and between children and adults (their mothers). From a Piagetian perspective, she argues that the development of moral reasoning would be assisted to a greater extent by interaction with a peer than with an adult because conflict between peers gives rise to an awareness that other legitimate perspectives exist. That is, in a relationship of equality, children understand that their partner has knowledge to contribute to the discussion. Furthermore, as most young children would consider that a peer has no social advantage, both have equal claims to the validity of their perspectives when working as a pair. From a Piagetian view, this forces children to integrate the different points of view into a common resolution. Accordingly, Kruger reports that after interaction with a peer, during which they had to reach consensus on two moral reasoning dilemmas, children demonstrated more sophisticated moral reasoning than those who interacted with adults.

The social processes that give rise to the benefits of the interaction are the discussions or reasoning transacts between the participants. A transactive discussion is defined as 'one in which an individual uses reasoning that operates on the reasoning of the partner or that significantly clarifies his or her own ideas' (Kruger & Tomasello, 1986, p. 681). Four types of transact were coded and applied to the discussions between peer participants:

1. transactive statements (other oriented),
2. transactive statements (self oriented),
3. transactive questions, and
4. transactive responses.

The results support the proposition that children's discussions with peers are qualitatively different from those with adults. In addition to the greater number of transacts overall, there was a greater number of transactive statements (other oriented) and transactive questions used by children working with their peers. In contrast, the number of transactive responses provided by children (in response to their partner's questions) was significantly greater in the parent–child dyads. Based on these findings, Kruger (1992) concludes that the symmetrical peer relationship facilitated the use of language that ultimately encouraged higher level moral reasoning.

Kruger (1993) develops the theoretical aspect of this research further when she discusses the mechanism(s) through which cognitive development takes place. What is it about social interaction that leads to successful outcome, namely higher level thinking or problem solving? Again, the debate Kruger engages in is conflict versus co-operation – in other words, whether a Piagetian explanation or a Vygotskian one is adequate. Kruger (1993) argues that the use of transacts or reasoned dialogues can aid in our understanding of the two seemingly discrepant explanations. Both explanations, she claims, rely on children encountering more than one perspective, and whether the situation is viewed as conflict or co-operation owes more to 'semantics than substance' (Kruger, 1993, p. 167). This may unfortunately owe more to a misinterpretation of Vygotskian theory than similarity of substance because the intersubjectivity characteristic of collaboration and co-operation, as discussed earlier in this chapter, does not simply rely on co-construction of individual thoughts to create a new perspective. Rather, intersubjectivity entails the formation and transformation of individuals' participation in the social interaction or social activity.

Nonetheless, Kruger (1993), using re-analysed data from her 1992 study, examines the notion that dealing with more than one perspective underpins both conflict and co-operation. Exploring the relationship between the type of transact and the solutions finally agreed on (and those rejected) for moral reasoning dilemmas, Kruger found that, contrary to predictions, only the discussion of rejected solutions is related to subsequent outcome. It had been predicted that children would co-construct solutions to the dilemmas, and that the parts of the discussion that focus on the solution ultimately accepted by the pair would be positively related to the outcome and post-test scores. This was not found. More specifically, the dyadic relationship and the discussion style related to the post-test individual scores of the focal children (who either interacted with a peer or an adult). Kruger describes post hoc two discussion styles: the egalitarian style, in which other-oriented transacts of both partners are combined, and the persuasive style, which combines the partner's information about the rejected solution, the focal child's other-oriented transacts regarding the rejected solution, and each partner's agreement with the accepted solution. Egalitarian style discussion of rejected solution was more frequent in the peer dyads but predicted outcome in the adult–child dyads and the whole sample. Persuasive style discussion is predictive of the focal child's post-test score in the peer dyads and in the total sample, but not in the adult–child pairs. These two styles can be presented schematically. In both cases, however, other-oriented transactive discussions are important. In the egalitarian style, the adult partner's transacts are highly relevant to the subsequent outcome; in the persuasive style, the peer's transacts are relevant. In each case, therefore, different conversational contexts are created for the focal child, but both lead to similar outcomes.

In summary, instead of characterising dyadic interactions as conflictual or co-operative, Kruger argues that, through the discussion of more than one possible solution, from two perspectives, the interactions are better described as collaborative. Such collaboration leads to greater understanding of the process and of the solution. However, improved scores on subsequent testing are not achieved through discussion of the solution finally accepted, but through discussion of solutions eventually rejected. Both styles, identified retrospectively, predicted the same superiority for discussion of rejected solutions. While the interaction process could be interpreted as supporting contradiction and disagreement as the means through which successful individual problem solving takes place, Kruger poses an alternative interpretation. She states that co-construction need not only involve joint creation of a solution, but discussion of individual ideas leads to higher levels of understanding of the solution and to a jointly arrived-at solution. Rejection of solutions was the variable that led to the achievement of a subsequent jointly constructed, acceptable solution, which in turn resulted in benefits for the focal children in terms of individual performance.

As noted earlier, it is my view that the description of what constitutes co-construction is not what Vygotsky would have construed as intersubjectivity, particularly as the focus of Kruger's research was still on the individual child. She did attempt to use the interaction as the focus of the study, but the research falls into the tradition of social influence. In this research, much of which has been interpreted by either a Vygotskian or a Piagetian perspective, or both, the individual continues to be the focus of analysis with the interaction viewed as an influence. The dyadic partner is the independent variable, as in the case described above, and the outcome for the focal child is the dependent variable. This type of research predominates in the problem solving literature, although it has not spawned any particular theory, conducive as it is to both theoretical interpretations. The *approach* is one of social influence, and the Kruger research is but one example. Others include studies by Tudge (1992), Teasley (1995), and Garton and Pratt (2001). Because the unit of analysis remains the individual and not the social interaction, a Vygotskian interpretation must be incomplete. However, because Vygotskian theory cannot explain and predict cognitive development, it is sufficient to describe the cognitive changes that are demonstrated by the experimental design and to illustrate learning, often but not always, in the less capable focal child.

The social influence view asks how the social environment affects an individual's performance and development, and how newly acquired skills or knowledge can be generalised. In contrast, the sociocultural view asks how individuals' roles and levels of understanding change as a consequence of their participation in social interaction, and how participation in one activity with one person relates to any other participation or activity. In terms of collaborative problem solving, these two views affect the object of study, the nature of the investigation, the data collected and the theoretical interpretations that are relevant and applicable. Isolating the individual enables the measurement of his or her knowledge and skills, and hence the charting of cognitive change and learning, and possibly cognitive development. Studying the activity is more complex, so it is easy to move towards studying the individual, despite the possible range of methodologies available for the observation and recording of shared activities and participation in joint interaction.

An illustrative example of research that has been conducted in a Vygotskian theoretical framework is that of Tudge and colleagues. Again we have the advantage of a comparative analysis, at least at the descriptive, if not the interpretive, level. Like Kruger's research, much of Tudge's relevant published work appeared in the early 1990s and acknowledges the legacy of the socio-cognitive conflict research conducted in the Piagetian tradition. Tudge (1992) points out the Piagetian-inspired research uses traditional tasks like conservation or spatial perspective-taking, which children are required to work on in peer pairs and reach agreement as to the solution. Subsequent individual testing allows for the assessment of the stability and robustness of the new level of cognitive functioning. By contrast, Vygotskian-inspired research has tended to focus on adult–child dyadic problem solving, emphasising collaboration and intersubjectivity. Tudge also reminds us that if partners who are to work together already share the same levels of understanding of the task, then there is no advantage for either party: it is the same as working alone. However, it is not sufficient for there to be differences in the level of understanding. There needs to be potential for change or achievement of intersubjectivity. This will not happen if one partner simply agrees with the other. A similar result would be expected if the levels of understanding were too discrepant. The implications of this relate to the assessment of the skill or knowledge levels of the partners of experimental interest, their pairings and the selection of the task used in the collaborative problem solving interaction.

Tudge was one of the first researchers to draw attention to the fact that, generally, the less capable child or partner in collaboration improves, but this is not a foregone conclusion. Even though, objectively, children may demonstrate differences to the experimenter's satisfaction in performance on a pre-test task, these differences may not be apparent to the partner in the pairing. Also, the differences are generally not made evident or explicit to the participants. Furthermore, the views of the less capable child might prevail in the interaction; even though intersubjectivity is achieved, an incorrect solution may be arrived at. Interaction could therefore be beneficial or deleterious to either or both partners.

That said, Tudge himself focuses on the consequences of collaborative problem solving with children of different abilities (higher, lower) compared to children working with similar ability peers and children working alone. Tudge used the balance beam task, based on Siegler's (1981) research on rule-based thinking in children. The task allows for the classification of children based on the rules they use to predict the workings of the beam, where each successive rule requires more sophisticated reasoning than the previous one. Seven rules were used based on the problems included in the study. Pairs were formed of children of different abilities but the same gender and from the same school class. The children ($n = 153$) were aged between five and nine years. The analyses were conducted on one member of each pair of high and low ability children, resulting in independent groups of more and less competent children. The type of pairing had a significant effect on post-test performances, with the group of less competent children being the only group to show significant improvement pre- to post-test. Interestingly, the more competent children showed a significant *decline* in performance compared to same ability paired children and those who worked alone.

Tudge discusses the decline in performance observed in the more competent children as a regression artifact. Because the more competent children were operating with a rule in advance of the less competent child, regression may not be surprising. It also depends on whether the regression was absolute (a shift downwards in the level of rule being applied and understood) or relative (within the dyad). Tudge discusses these alternatives when he couches his interpretation of the results in a Vygotskian rather than a Piagetian framework. He found that the former provides a better understanding of the data. The ZPD is a theoretical construct that allows for examination of the processes of social interaction. Instead of claiming it always creates a working area between actual cognitive functioning and potential future cognitive functioning, this study shows that the future level may be *behind* the current level, depending on the information provided by the partner and the acceptability of the reasoning supporting that position. Tudge notes that both regression of the more competent partner and improvement in the less competent partner occurred in circumstances where these children were successfully persuaded by the reasoning of their partner. Attaining intersubjectivity could lead to improvement or decline in cognitive development. Tudge thus extends an interpretation of Vygotsky's theory that permits the malleability of psychological functions so that development can be either facilitated or impeded.

Tudge tested for the stability and durability of the levels of reasoning attained (be they in advance of or behind previous levels) and found that the shared understanding achieved during interaction was maintained. Indeed he states that it was 'as though, as Vygotsky argued, the child's partner remained "invisibly present"' (Tudge, 1992, p. 1376). A useful caution is offered: the experimenter was at all times a third party in the social environment and, as such, even though his or her role was simply to set up the problem solving, may unwittingly have contributed to the outcomes. In particular, silence on the part of the adult experimenter may have been interpreted as affirmation of a correct answer. Even subsequent persistence in the solutions to the problems may have resulted due to the child's belief that the answer was correct, based on a misinterpreted cue from the experimenter.

Tudge concludes that, in accordance with both Piagetian and Vygotskian theories, his study demonstrates that social interaction, and specifically collaborative problem solving, can facilitate or benefit children's thinking.

The declines in performance, on the other hand, are not predicted by either theory. In order to accommodate this finding, both theories need some modification. Nonetheless, Vygotsky's theory appears more attractive to Tudge, even though, as I noted earlier, it is generally viewed as not accounting for regression. To account for regression means adopting the interpretation offered by Tudge, and this may not be in keeping with the philosophical underpinnings of the theory. Tudge argues that Piagetian theory is unable to account for regression because, he claims, children who hold particular views are more confident of their beliefs. This confounding of competence and confidence, Tudge argues, may have led to an over-optimistic interpretation of the benefits of collaboration.

In relation to the study conducted by Tudge (1992) and his application of theories to the data, we have an interesting comparison of Piagetian and Vygotskian theories and how each has been interpreted. Neither theory, in its generally described form, is adequate: Piagetian theory may have led to a confounding of competence and confidence being interpreted as illustrating improved cognitive competence, while Vygotskian theory requires emendation to the ZPD to incorporate decline in cognitive competence after interaction. Tudge invites replication.

Tudge's further work (e.g., Tudge & Winterhoff, 1993; Tudge, Winterhoff & Hogan, 1996) examines the role of feedback in benefiting the cognitive consequences of collaborative problem solving. Tudge and Winterhoff (1993) studied five- and six-year-old children as they worked together in pairs. The dyads were formed from a target child and a child who used the same rule in pre-test or a child whose rule was superior, and there were children who worked alone. The pairs were of the same gender and from the same classroom. Although the children seem younger than those usually studied in collaborative problem solving research, Tudge and Winterhoff were interested in discovering under what conditions children younger than six or seven years could benefit from collaboration. These are the ages around which Piagetian theory predicted children would benefit from interaction, as they have reached the concrete operational stage.

A major variable considered by Tudge and Winterhoff (1993) is feedback. They argue that both Vygotsky and Piaget recognised the importance of feedback for development. Piaget acknowledged the usefulness of physical feedback and included the resolution of conflicting perspectives as being a form of feedback that had benefits. Vygotsky, on the other hand, did not discuss feedback *per se*, but in his discussions of the benefits of social interaction it is obvious that feedback forms part of the establishment and maintenance of intersubjectivity. There was, they argued, a clear need to examine more closely the role of feedback on collaborative outcomes. So Tudge and Winterhoff designed their study to look at the effects of feedback from task materials on subsequent cognitive competence. The feedback took the form of letting children know if their answer, in this case their prediction, was correct. They also incorporated a longitudinal element, enabling the children to work together on multiple occasions. It had been argued by Azmitia (1988) that permitting children to work together on more than one occasion allowed them to develop a stable 'working style' that could have cognitive benefits. This line of argument is also relevant in considering the advantages – or disadvantages – of pairing friends, since friends are more likely than non-friends to establish rapport and greater mutual task engagement more quickly, either of which may facilitate subsequent cognitive competence. This is discussed further in Chapter 5.

A final variable in this study was the 'pegging' of the problems to be worked on collaboratively to the competence levels of the target children. That is, the problems were at the same level as, or slightly higher than, those solved successfully at pre-test by the target child, who then worked with someone at the same level or someone at a higher level – that is, using a more sophisticated rule – at pre-test.

Without going into detail about the careful design and analyses, this study shows that five- and six-year old children are able to benefit from collaborative problem solving but only under certain conditions. Target children who did not receive feedback but worked with a more competent partner demonstrated greater improvement than children in other groups. Overall, children who worked with more competent partners improved, but the improvement was greatest in the condition of no feedback. No benefits were noted from the multiple interaction sessions; children benefited quickly from the first session and the improvement was not only immediate but robust. This quick improvement can, in fact, be predicted by both Piagetian and Vygotskian theories, through accommodation in the former and by reaching the upper limits of potential in the ZPD during the first collaborative session in the latter.

However, Tudge and Winterhoff (1993) argued that stable working style, child's age and experience of school are confounded. So, for example, children with greater experience of school, but not necessarily older, used a more sophisticated rule in the initial individual sessions and also showed greater improvement at subsequent individual sessions. Also, children with greater experience of school (which requires the setting of working relationships with peers and teachers) benefited more from feedback. This links in with Vygotsky's theory, since schooling is a potent form of cultural influence. Schooling influences thinking and perhaps, it is speculated, encourages deductive reasoning and metacognitive strategies. All of these would affect performance on the type of reasoning task employed in Tudge and Winterhoff's study. Furthermore, when applied to stable working style, schooling may not relate so much to opportunities for collaboration as to development of understanding about particular ways of thinking or deploying knowledge. This again is taken as evidence for the applicability of Vygotsky's theory to explain improvements in cognitive competence under certain circumstances.

The study reported by Tudge, Winterhoff and Hogan (1996) is an attempt to answer some of the conflicting results reported by a plethora of researchers on the effects and effectiveness of peer collaboration on cognitive competence. Three reasons for the discrepant results were considered:

1. the role of feedback,
2. the type of dyadic pairing, and
3. the nature of the process of the interaction.

In many respects, this study was a replication of the previous ones discussed above, involving older children, aged six to nine years. Again, the balance beam task was used and children were assigned a level or a rule based on their individual pre-test performances. Both singletons and pairs were included, pairings based on children who used the same rule at pre-test, on children who collaborated with a more competent partner and on those who collaborated with a less competent partner. As before, children were matched on gender and classroom membership.

During collaboration, children were asked to take turns to make predictions about the movement of the balance beam under various conditions of weights and distances. After each made a prediction on a particular problem, each was asked to justify his or her prediction. When these predictions were in conflict, the children were asked to discuss these with one another and to come to a consensus. The experimenter left the room during the discussion to eliminate any artifacts arising from their presence, returning when agreement had been reached. Approximately two thirds of the children in each group were randomly assigned to a feedback condition in which they were advised by the experimenter of the correctness of their solution.

Again, we will not dwell on the details of the methodology, categorisation of children, coding of justifications and analyses. It is sufficient to report results of interest, while recognising that this simplifies what was a complex and thorough analysis. Overall, consistent with previous research and as hypothesised, children who received feedback improved to a significantly greater extent than those who did not. Again, children who worked with a partner improved more than singletons, but only when there was no feedback. For those receiving feedback, working as a singleton led to greater improvement than working with a partner, contrary to predictions. Also, not as hypothesised, and perhaps surprisingly, children who worked with a more competent partner did not improve to a significantly greater extent than those who worked with a similar ability or less competent partner. Finally, children exposed to a higher level reasoning, or whose partner supported their level of reasoning following feedback during collaboration and who adopted that level of reasoning themselves, were more likely to demonstrate cognitive growth. Feedback seemed to encourage higher rates of shared understanding, but shared understanding did occur spontaneously when there was no feedback. Such children were also more likely to show individual improvement later. It is hypothesised that this type of improvement was a consequence of selecting problems for the interaction session that were tailored to the target child in each pair, with the most difficult one being solvable by the rule above the one used in the pre-test. So problems for each pair were different, if tailored and arguably therefore limited. Tudge et al. (1996) argue that Piaget's and Vygotsky's theories would support this decision: that is, using situations that are capable of provoking conflict or of encouraging emergence of potential competence based on cognitive proximity. Children benefit from working on problems slightly in advance of their current capabilities.

Two factors are thus important – feedback and the relative competencies of the two children – though the relationship between them is not straightforward and may be mediated by the role of feedback. Furthermore, it is pointed out that working with a partner may not be the same as collaboration. This issue was discussed earlier in this chapter, but Tudge et al., noting that collaboration is usually interpreted as requiring co-construction of a joint understanding from alternative perspectives, suggest that perhaps something else in the interaction is influential. Somewhat radically, partners may actually distract one another from working on a solution to a problem. This may explain the relative success of singletons. However, it certainly is not a powerful explanation and has no theoretical basis. Another controversial point discussed again by Tudge et al. (1996) is the confounding of competence and confidence, which may explain the various patterns of improvement and regression.

Acknowledging the possible limitations of this study, Tudge et al. (1996) conclude that much of the discrepancy surrounding the benefits or otherwise of collaborative problem solving, and the mechanisms by which this process 'works', is a result of the theoretical perspective adopted in both formulating the experimental study and then interpreting the results. Their three conclusions are relevant to the broader debate at both a theoretical and an applied level.

1. Simply pairing together children who hold different views or solve problems according to different rules will not guarantee improvement. So ability level does not predict cognitive outcome.
2. Problems that are potentially solvable or that optimise mismatch between partners may be necessary but not sufficient for development. Children who arrive at shared understanding, or intersubjectivity, during collaboration are more likely to sustain that improvement when working individually.
3. Teachers need to be aware of both the benefits and limitations of children's collaboration as a teaching tool. There are advantages too for children working alone, particularly when feedback is given. Pedagogically, both strategies have pros and cons and teachers need to be aware of the situations where working together may be beneficial and when working alone may be beneficial, taking into account the variables examined in Tudge's program of research.

IMPLICATIONS FOR PIAGETIAN AND VYGOTSKIAN THEORIES

The work of Kruger and colleagues and Tudge and colleagues, mostly published during the 1990s, brings into sharp relief the various theoretical and experimental dilemmas that confront the study of children's problem solving, specifically collaborative problem solving. The studies examined in depth are illustrative and so are not exhaustive (indeed, many studies contemporary with and subsequent to those described above are discussed in later chapters), but they highlight, I believe, the critical issues debated in the literature on the relative explanatory value of the two theories. What these studies mean for discussion of cognitive change and, more importantly, for cognitive development – that is, the prediction of the development of knowledge – needs to be teased out.

So while there are similarities and differences, most published research on children's problem solving tends to adopt a theoretical position derived from Piaget's or from more recent post-Piagetian positions, such as that espoused by Case (e.g., 1985, 1992), or, more frequently, from a Vygotskian-inspired position. Why does the work draw so directly on these major theoretical perspectives, apart from the obvious explanation – that they are the indisputably fundamental theories for explaining developmental change in children and developmental processes? Social interaction is a process, and so it is inevitable that process accounts can at least shed some light on what it is about the interaction that aids learning or encourages developmental change. The theories are compelling in their explanatory value. But as we move away from a purely process account of the benefits of collaborative problem solving to examine aspects of the child as problem solver, Piagetian and Vygotskian explanations are no longer sufficient. Research, however, that has focused exclusively on the nature of the interaction has tended to rely on, or be informed by, Piagetian or Vygotskian theoretical explanations, and, in general, either is adequate, but there are important philosophical and methodological differences in the ways in which the research has been conducted. It can be argued that such differences are both a cause and a consequence of adopting a particular theoretical position. True scientific method commences from the adoption of a position that is then tested through a rigorously controlled experiment. In fact, in much of the collaborative problem solving research it transpires that either a Piagetian or a Vygotskian position could account for the findings. Take your pick! Most investigators find Vygotsky's theory more appealing, often because the method adopted, the task selected and the results reported can be explained by recourse to concepts embodied in the ZPD, itself a nebulous theoretical abstraction.

RESEARCH ON COLLABORATION: BEYOND SOCIAL INTERACTION

The work of Rogoff (for example, her 1998 chapter) provides an extension of this discussion because not only does she try, as noted earlier in this chapter, to tease out the similarities and differences between the theories, but she also identifies some major shortcomings of the research on collaborative problem solving. The shortcomings are related to work conducted in each of the theoretical positions, and she focuses on the lack of attention paid to the sociocultural factors in collaboration. However, by extending outwards the research that traditionally forms the focus of collaborative problem solving, we can find examples of work that borders on that which can be explained by sociocultural theories.

Research is often premised on the view that adults are the experts who support, scaffold, assist, tutor (the actual verb seems not to matter) children's learning. This detracts from focusing on the interaction, ignores the larger social and cultural aspects of the collaboration and may be the reason for the social influence perspective dominating research design. Instead of any of the alternative verbs suggested in the first sentence of this paragraph, Rogoff coins the phrase 'guided participation' (1990) to characterise the social embodiment of knowledge, specifically instructional communication between the adult expert and the child learner. In line with Vygotskian theory, instruction refers to both teaching and learning, and so guided participation recognises social participation and the contribution the novice or the child makes to the collaboration. Thus, attention needs to shift to consider the roles of both participants in the interaction during problem solving. Only when the roles are mutual can opportunities for learning be created. Opportunities for learning require partners to be able to adjust their roles and responsibilities to meet the levels of understanding of the other and to contribute to changing that understanding. There are large social and cultural differences in the extent to which either participant is involved in shared learning, as norms and institutions vary. School is often cited as an example where there are institutionalised roles for the expert, the teacher and the novice, the child learner.

The role of the expert, the adult, is to select suitable activities that provide relevant learning opportunities – although in reality, in developmental research, these are often chosen by the experimenter, hopefully with sufficient sensitivity – and then to make sure the environment is arranged to be conducive to learning. A role of the novice, or the child, is also to select activities. These activities are perhaps neither necessarily nor intentionally those that provide maximum learning opportunities, but they may be intrinsically interesting. They may equally be activities that have been mastered to a certain extent, but often in such circumstances adults can raise their expectations regarding the child's performance. The child makes choices about how to use the opportunity to learn. This may entail working out roles and responsibilities between partners, learning to use and monitor cues from the expert, and working out with whom it is best to work.

Rogoff cites the example of language learning as one where the adult takes a leadership role but encourages the participation of the child (see also Bruner, 1983). Infants' capacity to manage their own learning by establishing eye contact or smiling are examples of the novice taking a leading role and may, she conjectures, be the origin of intersubjectivity. In both cases, we are reminded that intersubjectivity, its establishment and how it changes over the course of the interaction, as partners work together to achieve a mutual and correct solution and children learn, is fundamental to a theoretical explanation that takes account of both partners and their sociocultural environment.

Peer assistance describes a process whereby, usually, children engage with each other and contribute to one another's learning. Research has typically been conducted with unrelated peers or classmates of similar ability, similar gender, similar age and, most likely, similar socio-economic backgrounds, but Rogoff points out that peers include siblings and neigh-bourhood groups. The focus of research has also typically been narrow, and has been confined largely to peer play, child caregiving, communica-tion in collaboration and classroom learning. Through illustrative research, Rogoff looks at areas where peers assist in the learning process, drawing on studies not traditionally reviewed. She includes cross-cultural work, cognitive conflict research (already discussed above and reviewed previ-ously by Azmitia, 1988, and Garton, 1992), studies on the 'community of learners' models of classroom and family relations and of instruction, and co-operative learning in the classroom.

Rogoff (1998) is keen to demonstrate that the 'sociocultural view through collaboration . . . extends far beyond the simple examination of the "social influence" of putting another person together with the indi-vidual child being studied' (p. 722). She reiterates the point that the col-laboration research fits the social influence model, at least in its design, while there are other social processes involving collaboration that extend beyond this limited view. A sociocultural view is not only consistent with Vygotskian theory, but it also gives rise to studies that consider the inter-action itself, how relationships are formed and maintained between par-ticipants, how individuals contribute differentially to solving a common problem or work jointly on an activity, and how these aspects of the inter-action 'are constituted by and themselves constitute cultural practices and institutions' (p. 722). Rogoff concludes by describing research that attempts to mesh the contributions of individuals with broader social and cultural contexts, drawing mainly from studies conducted in non-Western soci-eties. It is not of direct relevance to the central focus of this book, but suffice to say it draws attention to the cultural and historical aspects of collaboration and reminds us that cognition should not be regarded as sep-arate from all other aspects of development. Cognitive development derives from social processes and transforms as a consequence of participation in relevant cultural activities.

SOCIOCULTURAL THEORY

Contemporary sociocultural theory is only beginning to be applied to developmental psychology and children's cognitive development in par-ticular (Bearison & Dorval, 2002; Gauvain, 2001b; Hatano & Wertsch, 2001; Rogoff, 1998; Shweder et al., 1998). Sociocultural theory places the individual firmly in the centre of sociocultural activities and regards inter-action with others and 'cultural tools' as essential to the development of cognition (Hatano & Wertsch, 2001). Cultural tools are artifacts created at particular times in particular cultures that support cognitive activity. Westernised cultural tools include such things as clocks, street signs, dressmaking patterns, architectural plans and recipes (Gauvain, 2001a). Cultural tools also include such things as reading and writing systems and various forms of representational activity, as determined and shaped by the culture, usually via social means. Children observe adults using these cultural tools to obtain goals or to learn, and they gradually become tools that form part of the child's competence.

Earlier it was noted that the unit of analysis in sociocultural theory is not the individual but the interaction itself, although other areas studied include folk models, activities and situated cognitions and it is debatable whether these can all be subsumed under a common unit of analysis (Shweder et al., 1998). Indeed, Shweder et al. refer to the 'the unit of analysis problem' (p. 872), which they resolve through recourse to the notion of a custom complex (Whiting & Child, 1953, cited in Shweder et al., 1998). The custom complex combines mentalities and the symbolic and behavioural practices of a cultural community, hence combining activities and practices with mental activities. In essence, cultural or sociocultural approaches and theories take account of the broader context in which humans live and develop and link these to the development of mind or cognition. According to Rogoff (1998), both 'development and learning entail individuals' *transformation of participation* [her italics] in sociocultural activity' (p. 687). In this way, the roles adopted by individuals in any activity are not separate from the activity itself.

There are five characteristics of development and learning viewed from a sociocultural perspective (Rogoff, 1998):

1. There is an interdependence of individual, interpersonal and community processes; they constitute one another.
2. Learning can be regarded as the changing participation in activities that leads to individual change. Such participation is active and creative, and in a strong version of this view individuals can transform their understanding and role depending on the activity and can become people who can adopt various roles in society and in the cultural context, changing their understanding and their interpersonal relations. Participation in sociocultural activities can be flexible, dynamic and creative.
3. In Rogoff's (1998) analysis, she discusses where knowledge resides. In a sociocultural view, the development of knowledge comes from participation in shared activity, so knowledge is not static but arises as a consequence of cognitive transformation resulting from interaction. Understanding, knowledge growth and knowledge deployment are

dynamic, arising within the interaction as changes occur as a consequence of joint participation and involvement.

4. She comments that the distinction between competence and performance is not relevant to sociocultural theory as the focus shifts from what children can do (think or act) – in, say, certain experimental or natural situations – to what they are capable of thinking or doing. Developmental change, or transition as Rogoff calls it, focusing on the acquisition of individual competence, gives way to a focus on the roles of individuals in particular sociocultural activities. Change is qualitative, and varies according to cultural values, interpersonal needs and specific circumstances. As noted earlier, however, development *per se* is difficult to describe.

5. Participation in different activities does not reflect generalisation or transfer (which implies knowledge is stored); instead, the sociocultural approach recognises regularities in the structure of human activities.

Goodnow (2001) reinforces these views when she comments on a set of papers, published in *Human Development*, that all discuss the constitution of culture in mind. In other words, they are all focused on some aspect of sociocultural theory and analysis. She notes that four changes of direction underpin the research described in the sociocultural approach – changes that move away from a traditional view of cognitive development and align more closely with cultural approaches. Interestingly, she draws attention to an issue that pervades scientific endeavours and theoretical advances, namely the risk of 'replacing one one-sided approach with another' (p. 161). Adopting a sociocultural approach may lead us down the path of determinism, with the individual taking less responsibility for his or her own development and having less active involvement. In addition, embracing a social perspective can be negative as much as it can be positive and beneficial. These are useful cautions, and not just for the sociocultural approach but for any paradigm or theoretical shift. Indeed, part of the purpose of this book is to show that numerous theoretical positions can account for how children solve problems and the ways in which growth, development or change can be described, explained and predicted, and that there is no single prevailing paradigm or theory.

The four changes of direction, adapted to be pertinent to problem solving, are:

1. a move away from focus on the individual to the ways in which other people contribute to development, through structuring the problem solving situation for which competence is required, through introducing children to the availability of social and cultural tools and their

use and through introducing evaluative criteria against which progress can be judged;

2. a shift from the abstraction of cognitive competence to a consideration of the particular problem solving situation, which has the effect of encouraging an analysis of the situations or, in this case, the particular activity or problem;
3. adding value and identity to analyses of competence, thus integrating cognitive competence with other areas of development; and finally
4. viewing changes in individual competence as changes in relationships with others.

These four shifts away from the traditional explanations of cognitive development are reflected in sociocultural approaches. A further advantage of the sociocultural approach is that it moves away from the isolated individual and from a universal description of mind and its development. Somewhat perversely it allows for a study of individual differences, albeit within a social framework, moving away from a description of average, universal performances and competencies to a description that acknowledges differences between individuals, between activities, between situations and between cultures.

Gauvain (2001b) promotes the notion of cognition as a socially mediated process in so far as the social context indirectly influences learning. What resides in the mind and what is learned cannot be distinguished from the social and cultural processes that support such learning. Gauvain suggests that there are three agents of social change: the family, peers and what she terms the social community of development. Both parents and peers have already been extensively discussed, but Gauvain provides some examples of research where the social community, in particular schooling, provides a cultural or institutional framework within which children learn. The other examples of cognitive opportunities for children include daily routines, activity settings and social companions, each of which she illustrates in her chronological approach to social problem solving.

Bearison and Dorval (2002) discuss cognition as participatory collaboration in their sociocultural analysis of children's communication during problem solving. They take as their unit of analysis negotiations in conversational discourse. This is one of the very few studies to have used the social context and the process of collaboration as the unit of analysis and not the individual children. Furthermore, the study, instead of looking at outcomes or children's post-test learning, examined what was in the minds of the children as they participated in a collaborative task. The data of interest were the negotiations, or conversational turns, between children as they worked on a complex task, namely the co-construction of a rule-based board game. The monograph describes in detail the coding system used, the measures taken and the findings.

As the study was aimed specifically at looking in depth at the conversations between same-aged, same gender children, the sociocultural approach of using an open-ended task was considered appropriate. This approach is not focused on outcomes but on task-relevant communication, driven by the need to work together on an informal task with no specific 'correct' answer. The conversations generated are believed to reflect what the children were thinking, doing and learning as they worked together. The negotiations were coded along various dimensions, and it was found that different kinds of conversational turns were associated with different types of negotiation, and these were related then to different forms of evolving game complexity. Four kinds of negotiation – unresolved, acquiescence, acceptance and expansive – were recorded, reflecting increasingly constructive modes of interpersonal engagement. And increasing levels of co-constructed negotiations were associated with higher levels of game complexity. So, for example, expansive negotiations were the most developed because:

> they (1) were more likely to have occurred during planning phases of game co-constructions, (2) had a greater mean length of conversational turns, (3) had a greater proportion of elaborated conversational turns, . . . and, (6) subsequently were more likely than any other kinds of negotiation to result in methods of constructing games that advanced the level of game complexity. (Bearison & Dorval, 2002, pp. 108–9)

Overall, this study is one of the few to have taken the sociocultural approach and operationalised it in a way that enables the conversation between children to be developed from and to have an effect on the way the negotiations were constructed and their ultimate impact on the complexity of the board game that resulted. Even though different aged children participated, age was only a factor on measures of game complexity, such as numbers of conditional and constraining rules.

Bearison and Dorval (2002) conclude by extolling the benefits of this type of approach for the study of children's cognitive development. They contrast it with the study of conflicts and disagreements, and the consequences for individual outcomes. Instead they claim that the context they provided engendered mutuality and reciprocity among the children, which allowed each to learn. Furthermore, they link the approach directly back to Vygotskian notions of intersubjectivity as well as Piaget's social equilibration model, finding explanatory value in both theories. 'We found that coding turn-by-turn conversations between peers jointly participating in the co-construction of enactable board games enabled us to define sequential patterns of discourse that represented a continuum of developmental change from less to more complex kinds of collaborative cognition' (Bearison & Dorval, 2002, p. 120). This not only shifts the unit of analysis but can also be reconciled with two apparently different theoretical positions, while at the same time enabling the description of learning that takes place during collaboration.

DYNAMIC SYSTEMS

At a different level of analysis, Thelen and Smith (1994) discuss developmental principles that are non-linear dynamic systems, which lead to changes in structure and patterns. The underlying question is: 'What organic and environmental factors engender change for a human, developing in a complex world?' Development describes the route from an earlier state to a more mature one, via a 'messy' process that is context-specific. Dynamic systems theories try to explain common developmental elements that unfold in a diverse, flexible and asynchronic way. Thelen and Smith argue that such local variabilities are the processes that engender developmental change. The theory is biologically consistent but, it is claimed, not reductionist.

However, in common with a sociocultural view, the child is regarded as embedded within a dynamic system, albeit one that deals with perception and action. Goal-directed behaviours, such as reaching and locomotion, underpin the development of cognition. The human is regarded as a whole, a dynamic system. Experience is regarded as multimodal (Thelen, 2000), and future research needs to examine how movement is linked to things like problem solving. For example, when children work on jigsaw puzzles, this requires manipulation of the materials as well as the other behaviours typically regarded as fundamental to learning. Embodied cognition, it is claimed, is derived from the demonstration of links between movement and cognitive processes, as evidenced from work on a Piagetian task like the A-not-B error. The 'hard questions' of embodied cognition identified by Thelen and Smith (1994) are beginning to be translated into research (Thelen, 2000), which sees a future for the foundation of motor development to cognitive processes. For our purposes, this theoretical work is important because of the emphasis on the whole developing child and the integration of the physical, social and cognitive processes.

NATURE OF THE PROBLEM TO BE SOLVED

The study of problem solving in children generally requires:

- a task or a problem that has an achievable outcome, goal or solution;
- the deployment of certain strategies, skills or knowledge to reach or solve it; and
- other resources that may assist or impede in finding a solution, including other people (both physically and in terms of the knowledge and skills they bring to bear), existing knowledge and skill levels, and capacity to benefit from participation in the problem solving task.

In addition, the type of task set in problem solving research can affect the outcome and the way it is reached. Most research in the rubric of collaborative problem solving uses one of four types of task: jigsaw completion, using a model (Wertsch et al., 1980), model building (Azmitia, 1988), a balance beam task (e.g., Tudge, 1992; Tudge & Winterhoff; 1993; Tudge et al., 1996) or a sorting task (Garton & Pratt, 2001; Garton, Harvey & Pratt, submitted; Teasley, 1995). What they have in common is a capacity to vary the complexity levels, in a describable sequence, so the tasks can be used with children of different ages and abilities. Where they differ is in manner of presentation – verbal only (e.g., Kruger, 1992, 1993), manipulation of materials versus paper and pencil variants of proportional reasoning tasks (e.g., Tudge & Winterhoff, 1993; Reeve, Garton & O'Connor, 2002) – and the degree of familiarity children have with the format and materials (for example, many children have prior familiarity with completing jigsaws). This latter difference is important since it influences the ease or difficulty with which children can talk about the problems during interaction.

Most of the collaborative problem solving studies have not only varied the materials and/or the manner of presentation as well as the formation of the pairs (all of which make direct comparisons extremely hard and meta-analyses impossible), but they tend to use a pre-test/collaboration or interaction/post-test paradigm. This is problematic, as the researchers have not usually specified the nature of children's thinking before, during or after the collaboration (Siegler, 1996). The nature of thinking refers to the children's strategic and cognitive capacity while problem solving, either alone or in the company of others. This difficulty then interacts with the other issues related to the pairings, the materials and other design and methodological matters. For example, as many of the tasks used are conceptually ill-defined, it is impossible to measure or state with any precision any pre- to post-test gains – gains which are then claimed to represent learning. In the cases where conceptually well-defined tasks have been used, such as conservation tasks, only the presence or absence of ability can be tapped, and strategy use is difficult to measure. In some cases, such as Tudge (1992), the balance beam task allows for the measurement of learning but the studies have examined only the post-test outcomes and not what happens during the collaboration. Finally, and this is taken up in Chapter 5, apart from competence measures at pre-test, it would make sense to examine other attributes of the children, especially their propensity to benefit from social interaction or to take advantage of collaboration. After all, children will not all come with the same willingness, ability or inclination to work with another person.

HOW ELSE CAN PROBLEM SOLVING BE DESCRIBED AND EXPLAINED?

While most of the research on children as problem solvers has been conducted in a social influence framework and explained by Piagetian or Vygotskian theories, or variants thereof, there are other ways of looking at problem solving that do not necessarily invoke a social process account. The accounts described above, and the extension into sociocultural theories, all describe, explain and predict collaborative problem solving in relation to what happens to the individual child during the interaction. There are, however, other theories that can explain the improvements noted after interaction, whether expressed as learning, cognitive growth or cognitive development. None has the breadth or depth of explanatory power of the domain-general, or generally applicable, theories of Piaget and Vygotsky, but they can be applied to the child as problem solver. The following chapter addresses some of these issues to see if there is any explanatory value in conceptualising children in different, and measurable, ways and in re-examining the nature of the problems children are required to solve.

CHAPTER 3

STRATEGY USE AND LEARNING IN PROBLEM SOLVING

Problem solving can be understood in two ways (Garton, 1993): either learning and development are considered to be problem areas in their own right, or the focus – as in this book – is on children's ability to work out solutions to particular problems. This is an important distinction. Research on learning and development usually looks at the increasingly sophisticated strategies children have or acquire as a result of success and/or failure in solving a particular problem, such as language, music or walking. In a problem solving situation, children are presented with a task that has a goal and requires a strategy or strategies to reach the goal or to arrive at a solution. This latter approach allows us to consider some of the theories that have been proposed for the development of problem solving strategies.

DeLoache, Miller and Pierroutsakos (1998) use the analogy of the child as *bricoleur*. *Bricolage* translates as 'pottering', so, according to this view, the child is regarded as a 'jack of all trades', having no particular tools with which to reason about the multifarious situations and problems they encounter as part of their daily lives. Instead, they are equipped with a range of tools, not restricted to those directly relevant for the solution of a particular problem. So, rather than viewing children as having inadequate or incomplete problem solving skills and knowledge, they are regarded as being more active thinkers than adults and as having more heterogeneous reasoning capabilities, taking into account contextual information and prior knowledge. This analogy is useful for the discussion in this chapter, where the child as problem solver is considered in relation to various theories.

Clearly, as children develop, the nature of the problems they are required to solve changes. It is not sufficient to say the problems become more numerous or more complex because this may not necessarily be true, even though they are likely to increase in scope. However, and as noted in

Chapter 1, according to DeLoache et al. (1998), children's early problem solving is marked by opportunism and flexibility, but performance is limited by a number of factors. Among these is the availability of suitable strategies for solving a particular problem. As children develop, their problem solving must become more efficient and more reliable, since their worlds become more complex and it is parsimonious to foster systematicity in problem solving (and in other realms of life).

DOMAINS

What is a domain, and why are domains relevant for the study of problem solving? In the developmental psychology literature, a domain of knowledge is a set of interrelated principles (Gelman, 2000), the rules of their application and the objects and/or actions to which they are applied. The concept of domains was developed in response to the Piagetian stage theory of cognitive development and the notion of universality. Domains enable descriptions of the variability many researchers had noticed in the ways children learn. Instead of children's problem solving being the use and deployment of cognitive structures or schemas in increasingly complex situations or tasks (such as conservation, class inclusion) according to universal and biologically determined sequences, a domain approach postulates the acquisition of specific mental structures for particular tasks, activities or problems.

According to Gelman (2000), a domain as a set of principles guides and organises reasoning and learning in one particular domain as opposed to another. Domain specificity encourages paying attention to inputs that have potential to facilitate or enhance learning. In other words, 'they help learners find inputs that are relevant for knowledge acquisition and problem solving within that domain' (Gelman, 2000, p. 854). Examples of domains are arithmetical principles, biology and physical reasoning. As such, the object of knowledge becomes important rather than the application of general principles.

Domain-specific accounts of development (e.g., Carey & Spelke, 1994; Gopnik & Wellman, 1994; Wellman & Gelman, 1998) have been used to explain the processes of problem solving, mainly at an individual level but also for collaboration. Domain-specific accounts assume certain cognitive abilities are better suited for, or develop to deal with, particular activities or information. It is argued that young children do not have sufficient areas of specialised skill or knowledge to deal with every problem or situation they encounter. Indeed, in a domain-specific view, there are constraints on development that operate to affect cognitive growth, development or learning in the particular domains. Adopting a domain-specific approach means that the problem being considered becomes of utmost importance, and cognitive change can be identified and measured more accurately, both at the individual level and in collaboration. It can be argued that domain-general theories constrain the sociocultural processes and mechanisms in development, whereas domain-specific explanations can account for the apparently more general theoretical explanations.

Nonetheless, domain-specific accounts have been used in a range of areas of developmental psychology, most notably conceptual development (Gelman & Williams, 1998). In domain-specific theories, it is assumed that children select one strategy or solution over another due to limitations in those that are relevant for the particular task or problem. In other words, different problems or tasks require different solutions and perhaps different strategies for learning, and mental structures are constrained to select only those which add to that learning. What form the constraints take is debatable, but most of the theories use structural accounts, many favouring a modular account, others a biological one. Constraints can be regarded as both limiting and beneficial, since their limiting role can be interpreted as facilitating learning by reducing strategy selection. Domain-specific theories have not been so popular in collaborative problem solving research, probably because of the diverse tasks that have been used and the preferred emphasis on social explanations for cognitive change, learning and development.

DeLoache et al. (1998) distinguished between domain-specific, or knowledge-intensive, strategies and domain-general, or knowledge-lean, strategies. By making the distinction in this way, they are able to illustrate the types of problem solving strategies that are general rather than specific. General problem solving strategies include trial and error, means–ends analysis and what they term 'hill climbing'. These three types of knowledge-lean strategies vary in the cognitive load they impose on children, but each appears early on in a child's life. Knowledge-intensive strategies, on the other hand, impose a lesser cognitive load as they are tailored to the particular problem, and the nature of the problem limits the way the solution can be found. However, such strategies cannot be generalised to other problems.

In means–end strategies, children evaluate the difference between the solution or goal and the current situation and seek to reduce the difference between them. A good example is the task of assembling jigsaw puzzle pieces to resemble the picture on the box. There is not one simple, direct solution. Instead, the solution is achieved by working backwards from the final goal and setting sub-goals to achieve it. In the case of the jigsaw puzzle, a sub-goal may be to find all the corner pieces and, depending on the complexity of the puzzle, all the pieces that have recognisable shapes and which have a clear place in the pictured version because of their direct representation of an object in the picture. Means–ends problem solving is noticed across domains and imposes quite a heavy load on children as they are required to identify sub-goals and use them in a sequence to achieve the overall goal. A popular task requiring means–ends strategies is the Tower of Hanoi, in which discs of varying sizes are moved between three vertical sticks, from an initial configuration to a final one. The conditions are that only a smaller disc can be placed on a larger one and only one disc can be moved at a time. These limitations mean that the movement of the discs is restricted and children have to work out the moves to achieve the solution.

By contrast, trial and error strategies in problem solving involve trying solutions until a satisfactory goal or outcome is achieved. In children, trial and error strategies are often regarded as random, since problem solving is often conducted quickly and in no apparent order. Often too, children fail to keep track of which strategies they have tried already. So trial and error problem solving is characterised by a lack of systematicity. Because of their failure to evaluate process or progress, trial and error strategies impose a light cognitive load, but they are inefficient in other resources, such as time, and for longer-term learning.

Hill climbing again contrasts with means–ends problem solving because instead of working backwards from the goal, the child works forwards, selecting strategies that move him or her closer to the goal. Hence hill climbing – the selection of the path or route that will take you to the top the quickest. However, although it is relatively light in cognitive load, it does not always achieve the required outcome. As DeLoache et al. (1998) put it, 'Hill-climbing can result in the problem solver reaching a local maximum, that is a state that does not reach the goal but is closer to it than all other surrounding states' (p. 829). In addition, it carries a lighter cognitive load because strategy selection is limited to one at a time, rather than the child trying to order various sub-goals and strategies. Hill climbing also characterises the problem solving of young children, particularly on unfamiliar problems, which they try to solve using strategies previously tried and tested on familiar, less complex problems and then discover that the solution to the new task is not as obvious as they had believed.

In domain-specific or knowledge-intensive accounts of problem solving and learning, there is an underpinning of innate or core components, since it is difficult to argue for the recognition and use of relevant input when you start from scratch. While most domain-specific theorists would not support an innate view, as most have developed their theories to counter

Piaget's biological view of development, there have to be some domains that are core, privileged and universal. Gelman and Williams (1998) pointed to the following eight characteristics of 'successful' theories of cognitive development:

1. the sources of knowledge structures for both initial and subsequent learning;
2. how these structure encourage learning;
3. characterisation of the relevant inputs for initial and subsequent learning;
4. the sources of these inputs (and these include the social environment);
5. the nature of the child's participation in the elaboration of these knowledge structures;
6. the mechanisms of change from initial to subsequent learning;
7. variability in performance during learning, across tasks; and
8. the existence of cross-cultural universals of cognition.

As they observe, taking account of all eight characteristics is 'A tall order, to be sure' (Gelman & Williams, 1998, p. 599).

DOMAINS AS CONSTRAINTS ON COGNITIVE DEVELOPMENT

It is commonly hypothesised that domain-specific constraints operate to facilitate early learning in core domains. For example, children in infancy are able to engage socially with other people in their immediate environment, and this engagement leads to benefits. Furthermore, enabling constraints, as they are sometimes termed (see Gelman and Williams, 1998, for an extended discussion of this issue), continue to provide privileged knowledge and facilitate attention to and use of relevant information. So while there are universal or core principles, variability in performance and learning arises because the circumstances and environments in which the knowledge is manifested vary. Furthermore, different core domains require different types of learning, and there may not be any overlap with other domains. Domains can also vary in size and complexity, and there is debate in the literature about what actually constitutes a domain (Ferrari & Sternberg, 1998).

From this, it can be argued that children are constrained in their learning not by superficial, environmental characteristics but by universal structures. These core principles or structures, which are innate or at least internal, enable learning by restricting options and focusing attention on information that is relevant to learning in that domain. This argument has been extended by Goswami (1998), who suggested that privileged attention to particular aspects of the environment is the result of domain-general processes. This could include, for example, the role of social interaction as a facilitatory mechanism for learning, given an innate predisposition to use the social environment as an input that requires attention. It certainly does not rule out a domain-general account, nor does a domain-specific account necessarily exclude any role for the social environment.

INNATENESS AND DOMAIN-SPECIFICITY

Another way of construing domain-specificity has been put forward by Karmiloff-Smith (e.g., 1992). She includes a very large innate component in her theory of cognitive development, without, she argues, neglecting social and physical environments. Innate conceptual modules are the building blocks, the architecture, of the human mind. Again, the detail of what constitutes modules and the research debate surrounding their structure and function is not relevant to this book. What is important to acknowledge is that there is a large theoretical and empirical body of work that demonstrates and argues for the existence of innate conceptual processes, which work in specific domains, and that these modules constitute the human mind. According to Karmiloff-Smith, Fodor's (1983) position that innateness and domain-specificity constrain the human mind has influenced cognitive and developmental psychology over the past 20 years. In this view, the mind is constructed from genetically determined, independently functioning, special purpose input systems – in other words, modules. These input systems operate only on specific data and ignore others. This means they operate from the bottom up, and, because of their inflexibility, their initial manifestations may have a survival value for the developing child.

Cognitive science has largely been the driver of a modular approach to cognitive development, and much of the research has focused on the role of such input systems on information processing. Karmiloff-Smith herself has developed a variant of the strong version of hard-wired modularity, where she permits plasticity in the neonate mind. This is backed with evidence from developmental neurobiology. Such plasticity permits the development of modules, even if infants do come into the world with a limited set of modules to assist them to deal with the world. She argues that over time, 'braincircuits' (Karmiloff-Smith, 1992, p. 5) are selected for different domain-specific computations, which then give rise to encapsulated modules. This is regarded as gradual modularisation, although whether this is the case is an empirical question beyond the scope of this volume.

In discussing domain-specificity, Karmiloff-Smith (1992) defines domains along the usual lines of language and mathematics. However, she also distinguishes microdomains, such as pronoun acquisition within language development and counting in mathematics. She argues that she needed to make finer distinctions because of the phase model of development that she describes. She also draws on a broadly constructivist approach to development. While this may seem paradoxical, Karmiloff-Smith acknowledges that, in order to describe the complex interaction between the human mind and the environment, she needed to draw both on predispositions to knowledge in specific domains and on a theory that sees the child as an active constructor of his or her environment. This also links the theory to more domain-general accounts of development, while also allowing some focus on the outputs of cognitive processing.

Karmiloff-Smith's model of knowledge development is one of representational redescription. She discounts models of development that rely exclusively on innate components and models that take failure to reach a goal or adult advice as the trigger for new strategies, in favour of an account that sees humans exploiting internally existing (innate or acquired) knowledge. It is a reiterative or cyclical model, and representations are continually re-described 'by iteratively re-representing in different representational formats what its internal representations represent' (Karmiloff-Smith, 1992, p. 15). Through this process, implicit knowledge becomes explicit, moving from *in* the mind to *to* the mind: i.e., accessible and available for use.

While the process of representational redescription is domain-general, its manifestation is at the domain-specific level, since the level of explicitness of particular knowledge varies with the nature of the domain. So the process is the same in all domains while the content varies. In this way it is a phase model. Representational redescription occurs recurrently within domains (even microdomains) and characterises learning in children as well as new learning in adults. In Phase 1, children focus on the external environment for knowledge and create 'representational adjunctions' (Karmiloff-Smith, 1992, p. 18) from these data. These new representations are then added to the child's repertoire of representations in a domain-specific way. Children who are demonstrating Phase 1 learning or knowledge in any domain show success or behavioural mastery. However, such mastery is unlikely to be the same as adult mastery, nor does it imply representational mastery. Indeed, it is probable that the successful performance by children is a result of the application of one specific representation rather than the use of a more sophisticated and complex knowledge system. Karmiloff-Smith contrasts behavioural change and representational change to highlight this distinction.

In Phase 2, children are driven by internal data or systems, and internal representations generate change. Children's current knowledge in a particular (micro)domain underpins performance rather than any reliance on external data. This can lead to mistakes in performance and greater inflexibility, and may be manifested in less successful behaviour. It is important to note that any decline in performance is simply behavioural and not representational. In Phase 3, the child can deal with both external data and internal representations, they are reconciled and correct performance is demonstrated – the result of representational, not behavioural, change.

The internal representations that underpin these three phases are proposed to be at four levels: Implicit (I), Explicit-1 (E1), Explicit-2 (E2) and Explicit-3 (E3). These are neither developmental nor age related but are part of a reiterative process that occurs over and over again across domains and across ages in new learning contexts. At each level, a different representational format applies. In level I, representations take the form of procedures that operate on the external data. The following constraints are postulated for level I representations:

- information is encoded in procedural form;
- the procedure-like encodings are sequentially specified;
- new representations are stored separately; and
- these representations are bracketed such that neither intra-domain nor inter-domain representation links are formed.

Procedures remain as single, discrete entities, and there is neither linking with nor deployment in other domains. These remain implicit at this level, as does the knowledge residing in the procedures, and they require representational redescription (and developmental time). While the behaviour resulting from level I representations is relatively inflexible, there are advantages for the new learner to be able to respond successfully and quickly. The various E levels of knowledge representation reflect the subsequent reiterative levels of redescription. Briefly, level E1 representations are more flexible than those at level I, as knowledge is explicitly defined and available for use. They are, however, not necessarily available to conscious access or verbal report. At level E2, representations are available to conscious access, while it is not until level E3 that verbal report is possible. At this highest level of representation, knowledge is coded in a systematic way and in a way that is communicable to others through language (or some other code). There are multiple levels of representation of the same knowledge, and Karmiloff-Smith (1992) suggests that parsimony is not necessarily the mind's goal or solution; instead, the mind may be a redundant store of knowledge and processes.

Finally, for our purposes, a distinction between the processes of representational redescription and the actual representational redescription model is important. The process refers to the procedures applied to the external or internal data or knowledge, which cause it to be stored in a different representational format. The model as described so far postulates four hierarchically organised levels, but this is not the only possible model. There are several alternatives (see Karmiloff-Smith, 1992, p. 24), each of which could be supported by the same process of representational redescription. What is essential is that these representations are changed in a cyclical fashion and that they occur in different microdomains at different times, at different points in the learning process and at different ages. Maybe different models are applicable to different domains. This proposal (the model and the process) of Karmiloff-Smith's relies on learning being success rather than failure driven and representational redescription involving the stabilising of knowledge in a more accessible, explicit and integrated form.

DOMAINS AND THE SOCIAL ENVIRONMENT

So far, there has been little, if any, consideration given to the role of the social context within which domain learning takes place, possibly because, until now, the accounts explain solely how the child deals with the external data, namely the problem to be solved or mastered. Inputs that are attended to are defined by the structures of the domain, as noted previously, and the actual inputs themselves vary from domain to domain and from culture to culture and depend on the specific circumstances of the learning. In general, this means that during children's cognitive development certain universal principles or knowledge are acquired. This does not mean that culture-specific inputs exist and are attended to. In particular, cultures vary in the level and extent of social support that is provided to children in, say, the learning of language. The extent to which the social environment is attended to as a relevant input will influence the way in which the constraint operates and how the universal principle is learned. So, regardless of any cultural, social or environmental variations – that is, surface variations – structural and domain universals are learned. Which is not to say that the variations play no role because they can act to enhance children's learning or to assist focus children's attention on relevant input. Gelman and Williams (1998) also note other variabilities, including 'limits or differences in knowledge of conversational rules and task requirements, opportunities to practice, planning abilities and levels of knowledge' (p. 604).

In relation to problem solving, this points to looking at the particular task needing to be solved and describing, as suggested in Chapter 2, sources and patterns of variability and how these lead to learning. Instead of looking for universals, as evidenced through improved average performance with age, a domain-specific approach forces a different tack, which allows for uncovering structural core principles from variable performance, across tasks, across ages and across cultures. This approach also allows taking into account what may appear to be domain-general processes that can deal with variables such as social interaction or language use, which themselves can lead to systematic variations in cognitive development.

Domain-general theories of development are epitomised by the theories discussed in Chapter 2, namely those of Piaget and Vygotsky, which argued for universal processes in development. These universal processes may be applicable across such situations or tasks as studied by Piaget or across different areas of development such as studied by Vygotsky. In both cases, however, cognitive development and learning are characterised by measurable and qualitative increases in knowledge and more efficient ways of achieving solutions. In such accounts, the focus is predominantly on descriptions of cognition at any age rather than on how cognition develops or changes. This may be avoiding answering the 'how' question of cognitive development in favour of concentrating on the 'what' question, or else it genuinely reflects a lack of theoretical specification of whether biological, social, innate or learned factors can explain development. As discussed in Chapter 1, a great deal of the confusion can be attributed to terminological imprecision in the use of the terms 'cognitive development', 'cognitive change' and 'learning'.

STRATEGY CHOICE

A major source of variation in performance in problem solving tasks has to do with the strategies available and used by children. What are strategies? Most researchers concur that strategies are observable behaviours or describable principles that reflect children's past experience and present understanding of the task they are working on or the problem they are solving. The strategies used to solve any particular problem to some extent reflect the structure of that problem and how the problem is understood and represented by the child. As noted previously, strategies, particularly those that are domain-general, fall into three groups. Domain-specific strategies are more dependent on the properties of the task or problem itself and how these are construed by the child, in light of past experience, knowledge and learning. A related question is how children learn new strategies, especially in a domain-specific approach, since solutions may be unique to a particular problem or task. In the case of specific strategies, these may not be generalisable and children may never have the opportunity to re-apply the same strategy and to consolidate the learning.

Strategies can be regarded as evidence for children having multiple ways of solving problems and having options available when faced with different situations or tasks. Strategies are also taken as evidence for variability in children's problem solving and against the 'average' age approach to children's cognitive development. According to Siegler (1996), strategies for solving problems 'differ in their accuracy, in how long they take to execute, in their demands on processing resources, and in the range of problems to which they apply' (p. 14). Such variation in the strategies themselves means that through correct strategy selection children demonstrate adaptability and flexibility in their learning. Strategy learning and selection are two aspects of children's problem solving that require attention, since they form part of the support (knowledge, skills, social) that children have or can draw on to enable goal achievement. Strategies assist in focusing children's attention on relevant input information.

If research focus falls on the learning, use and modification of strategies in problem solving, then the experimental approach best suited is the microgenetic approach. This approach uses multiple observations of children with a view to identifying and describing patterns of change over time. This is in contrast to the standard experimental approach, which relies usually on a few observations elicited on one occasion, with many different aged children. This standard approach results in descriptions of levels of performance (often from 'inability' to 'mixed' to 'ability or achievement') for different ages. Microgenetic studies observe or tap children's abilities over a period of time (preferably when change is occurring, usually according to a preordained experimental manipulation) and thus describe individual differences and patterns in performance. The analyses consist of interpreting the nature of these observed changes in knowledge, in strategy use and in strategy development or learning. Many researchers have adopted a microgenetic approach, or a variant of it, and have, not surprisingly, identified a plethora of strategies within and between children, depending on the domain and the task.

We know that children have access to a range of strategies, but how do they choose between them? As noted earlier, the selection of a strategy is partly constrained by the structure of the task, and the interaction between strategy use and the task can lead to learning (Thornton, 1999). Looking at qualitative changes in children's problem solving, Thornton argues that, rather than cognitive development being constrained only by existing conceptual structures, there are other constraints in the form and nature of the task. The view that cognitive change is constrained by existing levels of knowledge is problematic, since the constraint can only apply to existing knowledge or existing cognitive structures and not to qualitatively different structures. It is acknowledged that conceptual structures do change, and this is brought about by altering aspects of a task to draw children's attention to certain input features that guide the testing of new strategies.

As part of her research, Thornton (1999) conducted a microgenetic analysis of discovery during a construction task with five-, seven- and nine-year-old children. It was assumed that at the start the children would not have an understanding of the principles required to solve the difficult problem she presented to them. The children were observed for a maximum of 25 minutes, and the videotaped problem solving sessions were analysed. Problem solving was segmented so that different forms of material manipulation were recorded as separate units (configuration), and, from these, sequences of configuration were identified. In this way, a range of sequences was catalogued, some representing only minor variations from one another and some reflecting a new way of solving the problem. In other words, approaches were identified in which a single principle was evident. In brief, children were found to use three strategies to solve the problem, and, within each, several sequences and configurations were noticed. However, only two of the strategies (or variants of them) actually gave rise to successful solution of the problem.

Changes in strategy use were noted, and within the session 63% of the children (mainly older ones) changed their initial strategy to a different approach. The five-year-old children showed less persistence in the task and greater resistance to change their initial strategy. It was also suggested that the older children who did change to a successful strategy understood the principle underpinning that strategy and why it led to the particular outcome or solution. This study demonstrates that strategy change can occur, and it was not so much that existing knowledge constrains the development of new cognitive structures, but rather that the task and its inherent structure (given that a fairly complicated task with several component parts was used) draw a child's attention to aspects of a potential solution of which they had not been previously aware. As well as using the microgenetic approach, by allowing children extended time to work on the task, the level of analysis was detailed and enabled the identification of strategies and strategy change. Success on the task was not the sole determinant of change, but a complex interaction of existing knowledge or conceptual structure, strategies and the task facilitates the development of new ways of thinking through constraining potential solutions and optional strategies. It is studies such as this that enable the identification of how children change the way they think, in the context of a problem solving task that both facilitates and constrains the deployment of new and existing knowledge.

Thornton's (1999) study looks at how young children learn new strategies in the context of problem solving. It is by no means the only study, nor is the framework she uses the only one in existence. Although not directly stipulated, the study was conducted within a domain-specific view of how thinking and learning take place. However, not only did she consider the input or the relevant information the child needs to consider when trying to find a solution to a problem, but she also pointed to the role that the outcome, goal or solution plays in the shifting of children's knowledge and hence their leaning. Taking the task into account (even if it is a structural explanation) means that the view held by Thornton straddles a domain-specific view and a view that considers the existence of broader environmental constraints. This is analogous to the position stated earlier, whereby domain-general principles can coexist with, or map onto, domain-specific principles. They are not dichotomous; other explanations are not ignored and can be accommodated within such explanations that take into account not only the domain of knowledge but also the culture, as exemplified here in the task but also noted in studies that consider the role of the social environment. Environmental constraints, it is argued, 'force' the child's attention on what to attend to, either through structural or social conventions, and facilitate or encourage the discovery or representation of alternative strategies. This could also be a description of learning, of cognitive change and even of cognitive development.

According to Siegler (1996), cognitive development is highly variable. It is precisely this variability that needs to be described and interpreted in order to improve theoretical developments in the processes of learning. Siegler uses two metaphors to describe cognitive development: the staircase metaphor and the overlapping waves metaphor.

The staircase model is aligned with Piagetian stage theory, and the assumption is that at a certain age all children behave in a particular way and that with increasing age these behaviours increase lawfully and quantitatively. 'N-year-olds are said to have a particular structure, a particular processing limit, a particular theory, strategy, or rule that gives rise to a single type of behaviour. Change involves a substitution of one mental entity (and accompanying behavior) for another' (Siegler, 1996, p. 4).

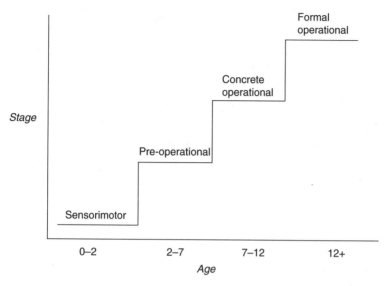

Figure 3.1   The staircase model.

Figure 3.1 shows the staircase. Children at a certain stage are on the tread of the staircase, and a shift in thinking is represented by a step in the staircase. The children then think at that higher level for a spell before rising up to the next step. It is a very simple metaphor and has been applied by others. Siegler cites, for example, Wellman's (1990) theory of mind model, which depicts the child as shifting abruptly at age three from Desire Theory to Belief–Desire Theory, a quantitatively higher level of behaviour and understanding.

The overlapping waves metaphor (Figure 3.2) characterises children's cognitive development as comprising a range of strategies or different behaviours over an extended period of time. Strategies come and go and represent multiple ways of thinking. Some of these strategies disappear only to reappear and be deployed more quickly. Alternatively, strategies may evolve from existing ones to meet the characteristics of a particular task. So, at any time, there are many strategies with varying levels of speed, accuracy, automaticity and breadth of applicability from which children can choose. This metaphor also shifts the questions researchers ask from 'What can children of a certain age *do* (or not do)?' to 'What sorts of strategies do older children use, why do they demonstrate qualitatively different sorts of thinking (be they quicker, more 'successful' or more accessible strategies), and how do they choose between potentially competing strategies?' Siegler, in pre-empting full description of relevant

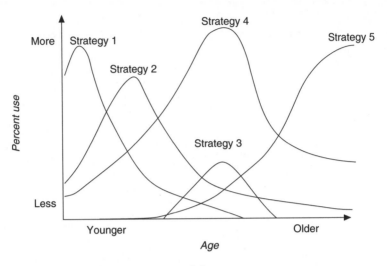

Figure 3.2   The overlapping waves model.

research, indicates that the learning of new skills and competencies is *the* most important task of childhood.

The overlapping waves model has widespread applicability, and Siegler (1996) gives examples of how it can explain development in the domains of arithmetic, locomotion, moral reasoning, social interaction and language. In each of these, where multiple approaches exist, change occurs in both the relative frequencies of use of competing strategies and in the use of new strategies and the disappearance of old ones. Furthermore, not only do new ways of thinking develop, but there are improvements in the speed, accuracy and automaticity with which strategies are used, and the range of problems that can be solved increases. Chen and Siegler (2000) use overlapping waves theory in their study of very young children, arguing that, while infants need to be studied in ways that are appropriate for their limited abilities, there is no reason why this model could not explain learning. The appeal of the theory lies in its explanatory power, tracking over time changes in the distribution of strategies used as well as the deployment of new strategies. The linear or sequential structure of strategic change in overlapping waves theory is applicable to the study of learning in infants and young children. The components of strategic change are, from initial strategy use to stable use:

1. acquisition of the strategy;
2. mapping the strategy onto novel problems;

3. strengthening the newly acquired strategy in familiar and new contexts;
4. choice refinement among alternatives; and
5. increasingly effective execution of the strategy.

This model and the theory were found to be useful to describe and explain the problem solving changes seen in toddlers, using a microgenetic methodology on a trial-by-trial basis, during which the young children had to retrieve an out-of-reach attractive toy with a suitable tool (from a selection), without any parental assistance. Chen and Siegler (2000) claim, through this study, to have 'crossed the divide' between work on learning in school-aged children and that in toddlers, through the use of a comparable methodology, model of strategy choice and theory of overlapping waves.

According to Siegler (1996), there are some broad principles that apply to strategy choice in all domains: variability, adaptiveness, change, individual differences and generalisation. These characteristics are derived from experimental work and also provide benchmarks against which alternative explanatory models can be evaluated. Variability refers to the use of different strategies within individual children to solve a problem. Adaptiveness refers to four ways in which strategy selection is adaptive:

1. Children choose strategies that lead to a quick solution or they decide to use a back-up one which may be slower but more accurate.
2. From back-up strategies, children choose the one that can be applied the fastest.
3. Children can react to changing task demands such as where speed or accuracy is emphasised.
4. Patterns of strategy choice are adaptive over time (both within and between problem solving sessions, for example), and with age.

Changes in strategy use are reflected in the availability of various strategies and choosing between them or using new strategies at the expense of superseded ones. This underpins efficient strategy choice, which in turn is linked with speedier and more accurate problem solving. The issue of individual differences in strategy selection is at the heart of the microgenetic approach, where patterns of strategies are described and various subgroups of, say, children, can be identified. This is a particularly useful way of describing age differences and cognitive changes over time. Generalisation is also an important characteristic of strategy choice, since the usefulness of strategies in successful problem solving can be gauged by the extent to which they are applicable to a wide range of situations.

Several models describing choice (in adults) are evaluated and ultimately dismissed by Siegler (1996). Rational choice theory, matching law models and decision-making models have all been applied to adult strategy choice but have limitations as far as children's thinking goes. In particular, these theories do not explain variability and change in strategy choice. That is, none of the alternative theories of choice (at least in adults) can explain variability in selection as, given certain task characteristics, each model will always generate the optimal solution. Hence, the models are also static. Therefore traditional psychological models of decision making and choice between alternatives have limited application to the study of children's thinking and problem solving.

Siegler (1996) offers three other explanations of strategy choice, derived from the developmental psychology literature. Metacognitive models have their origins in early studies of children's memory (e.g., Kail, 1979), in which memory strategies were examined in relation to how children remembered, retained and recalled material. Teaching children strategies that might aid retention of material gave rise to improved memory as seen in better (more accurate) recall. From this it was argued that making children conscious of the approaches that may benefit their memory was a strategy that could be applied more generally to other aspects of development and learning. The consequential models of choice were called 'metacognitive' because they require explicit awareness of how knowledge about memory can monitor and affect the way memory itself works.

Siegler (1996) proposes two models of metacognitive choice, each of which describes how explicit knowledge of a cognitive system assists strategy choice. These models typically include an 'executive function', which acts to monitor the system and guide rational choices. The 'executive' knows the limitations of the system, can analyse input and can guide appropriate strategy selection. An example of such a model is Flavell's (1981, in Siegler, 1996, p. 151), in which all aspects of the system are interrelated but only in a linear, non-hierarchical way, and metacognitive knowledge is not directly linked to metacognitive experiences. They are only linked through the actions and goals of cognition. Models such as this have been criticised as being too general to explain all cognitive phenomena, as the mechanisms are too imprecise. However, this breadth of potential applicability can be regarded as a strength, and certainly models (somewhat more sophisticated than Flavell's original conceptualisation) exist in the literature on cognitive psychology. Formal models allow for the development and testing of hypotheses about human cognitive processes in a range of areas such as memory, problem solving and reading.

The distributions of associations model (Siegler & Shrager, 1984) was developed to explain strategy choice without recourse to metacognitive processes or to explicit knowledge. It was derived from work on preschool-ers' strategies when solving problems of addition, with the aim of developing a formal model of how knowledge is represented for ultimate computerised simulation. In essence, the model assumes that the repre-sentation of knowledge contains associations between problems and potential answers, both correct and incorrect. The way problems are asso-ciated with solutions can be described according to various dimensions. Strategies or mechanisms work on these representations in a linear sequence, any of which may lead to an answer and each of which leads to changes in the representation. These processes are retrieval, elaboration of the representation and application of an algorithm. Retrieval is regarded as central to the model, which is a complex, mathematical model that permits predictions about performance during problem solving. The model can explain and predict strategy choice, how strategies change over time and why particular changes take place.

The third type of model developed and described by Siegler (1996; see also Siegler & Shipley, 1995; Siegler & Lemaire, 1997) is the adaptive strat-egy choice model (ASCM). This is a more flexible model of strategy choice with a different structure from previous ones, although it is still linear. Again, strategies are applied to problems to generate answers. However, the process also involves time and accuracy as well as a feedback loop, so that answers can influence knowledge about problems, which can lead to the generation of new knowledge as well as influencing the strategies used. So, during problem solving, children learn new knowledge about problems and new strategies. Again the model is reasonably complex, but ASCM includes a novelty element such that strategies can be generalised to unfamiliar, or new, problems, and it is also more flexible in so far as it is not reliant on three steps but allows strategies to be applied in any order. Instead of just focusing on association between problems and answers, ASCM includes speed and accuracy on new problems, specific problems, specific features and even on all problems. Instead of just choos-ing between retrieval and back-up strategies, as in the associations model, the ACSM allows for a wider variety of strategies to be selected and for generalisation to new problems as well as existing ones.

Siegler (1996) also evaluates the various models of strategy choice dis-cussed above against the five principles described earlier. The metacogni-tive models are shown to be inadequate for explaining children's strategy choice, and indeed this failure was the impetus for the development of the associations model. Although claimed by Siegler to be of greater utility when describing children's learning, this model cannot, in any straight-forward way, explain how new strategies are assimilated into the process of strategy choice. That is, the model can explain choice from among competing strategies but not how new ones develop and become available for selection. So the model can be regarded as being relatively inflexible. The three phases, even though they are recurrent, were soon shown to be too restrictive, even if applicable to children learning addition. Again, the limitations were the impetus for the next model. The major limitation of the ASCM, however, is its failure to account for the development of new strategies apart from through the modification of existing ones. The issue of learning new strategies is discussed in the next section.

A fourth model, SCADS (strategy choice and discovery simulation) has recently been developed by Siegler and colleagues and has only been used in computer simulations (Shrager & Siegler, 1998). As noted earlier, a goal of Siegler's research has not only been the verification of the overlapping waves theory of children's learning through an examination of models of strategy choice, but also the development of computer simulation models that can describe and explain cognitive development. Siegler (2000) notes that, through computer simulation, the overlapping waves model has been shown to be derived from several learning processes. With experience, there is an 'increasingly extensive database' (Siegler, 2000, p. 29) associated with problems and strategies. This information relates to the speed and accuracy of each strategy in solving problems in general, specific problems and problems with particular features. With experience, each strategy becomes more automatic. As the database increases in size and scope, children have more strategies from which to choose, so choices become more refined and selection can be made of the most advanced strategy. This means that problem solving becomes more effortless as well as fast and accurate.

SCADS (Shrager & Siegler, 1998) also allows for the discovery of new strategies that arise through an interplay of metacognitive and associative processes in learning. Briefly, with increasing automatisation in the selection and use of strategies, cognitive load is reduced, freeing up resources that had previously been part of executive processes (such as monitoring). These newly freed-up resources are then used to look for redundant processing in existing strategies, and 'If such redundancies are found, strategy discovery heuristics are used to generate potential strategies from the components of previous ones . . . [which] are then evaluated against conceptual constraints on legitimate strategies' (Siegler, 2000, p. 29). With increasing use, speed and accuracy improve, and, as newly discovered strategies become more efficient, they replace existing ones. Interestingly, Siegler acknowledges that any model explaining learning needs to have both a metacognitive and an associative component, since this is the way children's thinking develops. 'Focusing on one to the exclusion of the other yields a one-sided picture of cognitive growth' (Siegler, 2000, p. 30).

Kuhn, Garcia-Mila, Zohar and Andersen (1995) examined knowledge acquisition with two different age groups of children. The main thrust of this research was to illustrate how knowledge is acquired through the coordination of children's theories with new evidence. This, it is claimed, contrasts with the usual view that neglects how theories are formed and revised in favour of describing children's evolving theories in particular domains. Using the microgenetic approach, Kuhn et al. embarked on a demonstration of how children's strategies or knowledge vary within and between individuals and also developmentally. So instead of assuming that these strategies do not vary with age, the research aims to show explicitly that children's theories, or knowledge strategies, are capable of variation. Kuhn et al. did not limit the options available for children to select the evidence on which they based their thinking – in this case, their inferences. This links the research work to scientific reasoning as exemplified by the development of inductive reasoning strategies.

The microgenetic method further facilitates this type of approach, since changes over time can be described and those changes are initiated by the children while they work with the experimental materials. In an elaborated form of the method, Kuhn et al. (1995) simultaneously tracked two types of change over time within a domain: the child's evolving knowledge within the particular domain, and changes in strategies of knowledge acquisition. These latter changes may evolve as knowledge itself is acquired. Furthermore, change was observed in the multiple domains in which the child was engaged concurrently. This enabled examination of knowledge acquisition and strategy use across domains as well as permitting comparisons of within-domain change. Also, the elaborated microgenetic method was designed to include a transfer element to examine the generalisability of the knowledge acquisition strategies. Finally, the design was repeated with different aged participants – pre-adolescent children and adults – to compare knowledge acquisition processes across ages. This again addresses the generalisability issue, but across samples rather than content.

Placing the research in the context of previous work allowed Kuhn et al. (1995) to draw on a wide range of research endeavours, stretching from traditional learning theory to metacognition, from scientific reasoning to causal inferences, and from studies of the origins of beliefs to strategic competence. The main tenet is that individuals are constrained in how and what new knowledge they acquire by the level of their existing knowledge. Furthermore, while studies have tended to be domain-specific, it is important to describe the organisation of theories across domains, in order to be able describe the architecture of knowledge. However, taking that into account, Kuhn et al. proposed to study the actual mechanisms of cognitive change by looking directly at individual processes accelerated through the microgenetic design. Forcing individuals to make changes allows experimenters to observe those changes and to describe individual variability. Instead of looking for average changes in a group, manufactured by the experimenter, this approach encourages diversity through individual strategy choice. The only constraint is the individual's existing knowledge. Of course, the actual domains for study are chosen by the researchers, but the selection will usually enable generalisation, or, to put it another way, it will allow researchers to study the contrast between domain specificity and domain generality. While this does not enable the study of transfer, it does allow the researcher to see if strategies across tasks develop or are deployed concurrently, simultaneously or successively.

Kuhn et al. (1995) studied pre-adolescent children and a similar number of adults. Two domains were investigated – the physical domain and the social domain – with two problems in each. Participants attended for two 30–45-minute problem solving sessions per week for ten weeks. The existing theories held by the participants were explored in the first session, revisited briefly at the end of each session and in depth again at the end of the final session. The actual problems had an 'isomorphic' structure (Kuhn et al., 1995, p. 26), with two of the five features in the problem having no bearing on the outcome, and, of the remaining three, one had a causal effect, one an interactive effect and the last a curvilinear effect. These features were always discussed explicitly with the participants before they were asked to use the evidence to explore outcomes. Notebooks were provided so participants could keep track of their strategies, if they so wished. The data of interest were the qualitative indicators of theory change as seen in the theories espoused by the individual while working on the problems. In particular, focus was on the differences between initial and final theories for any specific feature, and these differences formed an index of knowledge acquisition. The other data were quantitative and were derived from individuals' evolving ability to predict the actual outcomes.

It is impossible to do justice to this study, especially as it is reported in a monograph and is therefore an extensive piece of research. At its heart is the careful description of theory development and theory change and how knowledge is acquired in a developmental context. Consistent with the general approach, large individual variability in strategy use is documented for both the children and the adults. In other words, all participants displayed a range of different strategies and employed them both selectively and variably across the problem solving sessions. This is interpreted as showing that variability is characteristic of cognitive functioning and is not confined to children or to times of cognitive transition. In addition, such variability highlights the importance of assessing cognitive ability on more than one occasion, enabling a frequency distribution of performance over time and hence a more accurate picture of actual strategy use than that obtained from once-only assessment. Kuhn et al. (1995) point out, however, that even strategy use over time could be a misleading characterisation since, over time, individuals' strategy use evolves and less adequate strategies are used less frequently. Improvement is not constant; instead performance usually levels off as individuals become less engaged and less motivated. So, because engagement levels vary with different tasks, it is recommended that later strategy use rather than earlier strategy use be taken as a measure of cognitive competence.

A second feature of the results is that variability was noted across domains. Assuming that the strategies deployed on one task are but a subsample of all available strategies, and the introduction of a second task also allows use of a range of strategies, then it is inferred that this variability is a function of the participant (in contrast to the usual view of décalage, where variability is a function of the task content). The implication is that cross-task strategic variability is constrained by intraindividual within-task strategic variability. The patterns of strategy transfer also reflect individual variability, and the introduction of a transfer task enabled the demonstration of another range of strategies.

Although individual variability in strategy used was noted in general, there was evidence of domain specificity, and, for example, performance was poorer on the problems in the social domain than in the physical domain. An interesting distinction between different sorts of generality that Kuhn et al. (1995) make is reflected in generality in the applicability of strategies, generality in the competence to use these strategies and generality in their actual application. Applicability is a non-empirical question, since the tasks were selected by the experimenter. Competence to use and application are empirical issues, which are studied to a certain extent in the monograph. These issues are further related to cognitive change, and evidence suggests that, while changing knowledge was limited to a particular domain, strategy use was more general and variable.

So what does change? Kuhn et al. (1995) suggest that microgenetic analyses rather than age-related comparisons provide the necessary evidence for differences between initial starting levels of performance and final levels of attainment. This difference reflects cognitive change. Both adults and children displayed improvement over time, and both groups used a range of strategies, but, in general, adults performed better than children. Adults were able to benefit more from their greater knowledge and skills. Knowledge acquisition was shown to be a process of coordinating both new and existing knowledge – called 'theory-evidence coordination' by Kuhn et al. (1995, p. 107). Children's performance, their 'comparative deficiencies' (p. 111), was a result of poorer strategic competencies. They did, however, show a similar path in their cognitive progress to the adults.

LEARNING NEW STRATEGIES

In another aspect of his research program, Siegler looks at novel strategy learning and generalisation of strategies in young children, as opposed to computer simulations. Siegler (1996) discusses the development of new strategies when children work alone and when they work collaboratively. The child as solitary problem solver must figure out a new strategy as well as working out how to choose it over existing alternative ones. Using microgenetic methods, Siegler and colleagues were able to analyse changes in the way individual children acquired a new strategy for adding together small numbers (e.g., Siegler & Jenkins, 1989). In particular, the role of feedback for the learning and use of new strategies was considered important, as was whether learning was specific to problems or more general across different sorts of problems. Without going into too much detail, it seems that, because of the nature of the problem to be solved, solution strategies could be generated by the research team in advance (and used in the computer simulations) and children's varying solutions mapped onto these according to a logical progression. Children who did not already demonstrate the strategy of interest were also studied. Siegler (1996) describes in depth how such a strategy can be found, used, generalised and understood. He also proposes that strategy generation is constrained by a 'goal sketch', which specifies the hierarchy of objectives that a satisfactory strategy must meet. This hierarchy directs the child to search existing knowledge for sub-procedures that meet the current goal (even if these are part of separate procedures). This directs the search away from strategies that violate the principles of the current problem. Siegler and Jenkins (1989) did not observe any child using a strategy that was illegitimate in that it violated principles or did not meet the goals. So a constraining mechanism is hypothesised to restrict the alternatives when new strategies are being developed or when learning is taking place.

A further way new strategies can be developed is through explicit training. Training was studied extensively in the 1970s in relation to Piagetian tasks to see if conservation, class inclusion and so on could be taught. In more recent times, Siegler (1995) has used conservation in microgenetic studies to examine the notion that strategies are acquired gradually, even when children are able to give reasonable explanations of why the new strategy is better than the one used previously. Training non-conserving children took various forms:

- correct or incorrect feedback;
- feedback plus a request for an explanation from the children; and
- feedback plus the experimenter asking 'How do you think I knew that?'

This last question was of greatest research interest and led to the greatest cognitive gains compared with the other conditions. The usefulness of receiving feedback, together with the child showing knowledge of the experimenter's reasoning, leads into both collaborative problem solving (since another person is involved) and further research into the potential benefits of being aware of the knowledge held by the other person in collaborative problem solving.

Crowley and Siegler (1999) looked at the generalisation of individual children's strategy learning. This study started from the premise that one way children learn new strategies is through observation of others. However, learning through observation does not allow for the strategy to be explained. While this may not be necessary when problems require identical solutions to be correct, explanation and understanding are usually necessary in other situations. Generalisation can be facilitated by different types and different amounts of explanation as well as having opportunity to think about more advanced strategies than those currently being used by children. Crowley and Siegler's study took this one step further in looking at how facilitation occurs. Three explanations for the generalisation of strategies were offered and tested:

1. explanations make procedures in the strategy easier to recall;
2. explanations give the strategies privileged status over existing strategies; and
3. explanations make it easier to keep track of sub-goal execution in the strategy.

The study involved a tic-tac-toe problem and six-, seven- and eight-year-old children. Children participated in a pre-test, the study of example problems, a generalisation post-test and a recall post-test. The three mechanisms by which generalisation may take place were assessed through behavioural measures. In short, the third mechanism was found to be most efficacious for learning. Children who memorised the initial sub-goals of the strategy almost always recalled them and chose to use the new strategy in the generalisation phase, regardless of whether they could explain the new strategy. However, children who knew the explanation were better able to resist attempts to abandon it in favour of earlier or easier strategies. While this study showed the benefits to children's learning of memorising sub-goals, it also showed there were benefits to having knowledge of the explanation. The task used is a fast-moving one requiring flexible thinking, characteristics of everyday thinking but not necessarily of arithmetic, for example. So further research in other domains is still required.

Collaborative problem solving is dealt with in passing by Siegler (1996), who comments, 'Attempts to specify when collaboration helps learning have been hampered by lack of precise assessment of children's thinking before, during, and after the collaboration, and of the social interaction that went on during the collaboration' (Siegler, 1996, p. 210). While this judgement is perhaps a bit harsh, since there has been considerable work looking at features of the interaction (discussed in Chapter 4), it is true that work has only recently begun to pay greater attention to the former, and this will form the basis of Chapter 5.

Kuhn et al. (1995) believed that their experimental support for intra-individual variability in strategy use complicates any explanation of strategy development or learning. Because at any one time an individual has a range of strategies available and the probability of their use is variable, developmental change can be characterised as change in the respective strength of each strategy. A new strategy emerges with an increase in strength of zero, while an old strategy decreases in relative strength back to zero. Zero does not mean absent. Dynamic systems models of change capture these complex changes. As Kuhn (1998) notes, in cognitive development we see shifts in the distribution of strategy use. In learning new strategies, microgenetic use of strategies leads to change, but such practice can also enhance awareness of these strategies. Such awareness (or metastrategic knowledge) can both guide and follow strategic development itself. But change is not triggered by a simple instance of discrepant feedback, since such feedback does not necessarily lead to change or to correct strategy use resulting in cognitive change. Kuhn et al. (1995) draw attention to social factors that assist in strategy learning. In particular, they point to the powerful role of dialogic reasoning that could occur in collaborative learning. In social problem solving, where individuals work together, dialogic reasoning is encouraged and inter-individual discussion draws out differences in content and strategic knowledge. Such discussion and debate can, according to Kuhn et al., lead to new levels of understanding in both participants. Some of this work will be described in Chapter 4.

CHAPTER 4
SOCIAL PROBLEM SOLVING

In Chapter 2, I examined various theoretical perspectives that have been used to describe and explain children's cognitive development and learning during and after collaborative problem solving. Some studies were discussed that illustrated theoretical positions advanced by Piaget and Vygotsky, respectively – notably those on peer collaboration conducted by Kruger (1992, 1993) and by Tudge and colleagues (e.g., Tudge, 1992; Tudge & Winterhoff, 1993; Tudge, Winterhoff & Hogan, 1996). These studies were set in the context of the view that theory influences the research question asked (e.g., Van Meter & Stevens, 2000) and the way the research is designed, analysed and interpreted. In a synthesis of some papers published in a special issue of *The Journal of Experimental Education*, Van Meter and Stevens (2000) argue, on the basis of the studies in that issue, that an integrated theory of collaborative process can be constructed. In such a theory – or framework, as it incorporates various theoretical perspectives – it is proposed that contextual factors differentially affect discourse structure, which in turn affects learning outcomes. Both Piagetian and information-processing theories offer the best explanation of collaborative processing. Individual differences, in particular gender and prior knowledge, influence the way the groups collaborate and the type of discourse. Individual differences are discussed at greater length in Chapter 5.

This chapter takes as its starting point the position that social interaction in various guises influences children's cognitive development, cognitive change and learning. Not that theory is unimportant, but in this chapter I seek to discuss various forms of social problem solving research (parent–child, peer) conducted in relation to various theoretical frameworks, including those of Piaget and Vygotsky. The major aim is to demonstrate and recognise the great diversity of approaches that have been taken (and legitimately so) in problem solving research. It is not necessarily my intention to integrate these theories, as, firstly, this may not be possible given the diversity of approaches and, secondly, it may not be helpful or theoretically illuminating to do so. A diverse range of theories and explanations leads to different research questions being asked and, arguably, a greater richness of research.

Social problem solving is defined as problem solving that takes place in a social context, be it pairs or groups. Collaborative problem solving research has typically been conducted with children working in pairs (often termed dyadic interaction), although some has used small groups (Doise, 1978; Perret-Clermont, 1980). While a large body of research has considered children working in groups (e.g., Webb, 1989; Webb & Favier, 1999) or peer tutoring, the focus of this work has not always been specifically on problem solving *per se*.

DeLoache et al. (1998) discuss group problem solving, but focus almost exclusively on scaffolding and peer tutoring. They start from the notion that the social regulation of problem solving is an important component in both the ZPD and in scaffolding (see Chapter 1). In both cases, the role of the 'tutor' is stressed, and research focus is on how or to what extent the tutor is sensitive to the current level of the child and hence provides planning and monitoring to aid in cognitive development. Children are qualitatively different tutors from adults and are more direct rather than providing the planning support. Citing researchers such as Teasley (1995) and Radziszewska and Rogoff (1991), whose work involved dyads, DeLoache et al. claim that these studies of peer tutoring show the extent to which the child can take an active role in the tutoring process. This tutoring role varies according to the relative status and expertise of the tutor (for example, expert peers, novice peers or adults), the teaching style(s) adopted by the tutor and how well the tutor adapts to the level of the tutee.

While these studies are interesting examples of peer tutoring, they are not examples of research looking at *group* processes during social interaction. Instead, they are instances of where groups may assist one another. The research enterprise, however, has been largely devoted to the study of various dyads. Dyadic peer interaction is a form of social problem solving, and it is the one to which I intend to direct most attention, even though peer interaction can incorporate both dyadic and group processes. The central focus is on children working with peers in pairs or in groups, or in comparison with other forms of dyadic interaction.

PEER INTERACTION AND PROBLEM SOLVING: A THEORETICAL CONUNDRUM

Peer interaction, as noted above, is usually confined to instances where either pairs of children or small groups of children (between three and five in number) work together to solve problems. Various comparisons are then made:

- with different interventions within or between pairs or groups,
- with other pairs such as adult–child dyads,
- with control children who do not have the benefit of intervention,
- between or within different types of problems, or
- between different theoretical interpretations.

This gives rise to a huge diversity of research, which is difficult to summarise, let alone synthesise. I intend to give illustrative examples of the range, using published research, that has tackled the issue of how children develop knowledge or cognition through problem solving. The starting points of these various research studies are not always the same, and the research questions vary, but in each case either a Piagetian conflict-type interpretation or a Vygotskian social and cultural interpretation has been used to explain some, if not all, of the results.

Druyan (2001) examined the role of cognitive conflict on children's problem solving. Conflict was created in four ways – two physical, either visual or kinaesthetic, and two social, either peer conflict or child–adult conflict. In the physical conflict conditions, children were presented with visual evidence of their prediction on Siegler's (1976) balance beam task. In the kinaesthetic condition, after making his or her prediction, the child was able to pick up the balance beam by a loop tied to the fulcrum to sense the movement of the beam after the wooden blocks holding each end in place were removed. In the peer conflict condition, children were assigned to pairs, each of whom had a different level of understanding of the balance concept as assessed at pre-test. When individual predictions varied, the children were encouraged to discuss their solutions and to come to an agreed position. Child–adult conflict was generated by the experimenter providing the child with verbal feedback about his or her predictions, both correct and incorrect, and giving justification of the opinion. A fifth group of children comprised the control group. Children were aged between five and twelve years, and a pre-test/intervention/post-test design was used.

In terms of developmental trends in levels of understanding on the balance beam task, children showed that as they got older they were more able to solve complex problems and to predict successfully the movement of the balance beam as a function of the weights attached and of their distance from the central fulcrum. Children in third and fifth grades showed that they were, in general, able to make correct predictions on both dimensions but were not able to coordinate both or to solve complex problems.

An interaction was found between the age of the child and the type of conflict that led to a higher level of performance at post-test. For young kindergarten-age children, physical conflict (mainly the kinaesthetic kind) was more effective than social conflict in leading to improved performance, while for the school-age children (both grades), the social conflicts were more effective, particularly those involving adult–child conflict. As the study was aimed at examining the 'ideal' conditions for facilitating intrapersonal conflict and hence cognitive change, Druyan (2001) claims that the study demonstrates an interaction between the age of the child and the effective type of conflict. She interprets this as supporting Piaget's position *as well as* Vygotsky's. From Piaget she draws on the development of scientific reasoning and the role of physical conflict in the younger children. The argument put forward by Piaget – that children cannot benefit from social interaction until they have reached the operational stage and can decentre effectively – is invoked to support this argument further. From Vygotsky, Druyan argues that the study also supports an interpretation that interaction with cultural objects, in this case the balance beam, enhances cognitive development. In addition, Vygotsky's theory would support the increasing role played by social interaction, particularly adult–child interaction, where adults model new knowledge and lead the child through the ZPD. So, according to this study, both theories are possible frameworks for explaining what goes on when cognitive conflict is induced and what types of circumstances lead to cognitive development.

Kruger (1993) asks the question 'Peer collaboration: conflict, cooperation or both?' and draws attention to the processes of peer interaction and the outcomes in terms of cognitive change. From a problem solving perspective, children were solving story dilemmas dealing with fairness, sharing and distributive justice. As noted in Chapter 2, this paper by Kruger attempts to place her work on the role of transactive discussions on facilitating children's cognitive development in the context of theories that emphasise conflict, cooperation and/or collaboration. Like Druyan (2001), this paper attempts to illustrate how both theoretical perspectives can account for cognitive change following some sort of discussion between dyads or groups, between peers and between adults and children.

Some of the apparent confusion in the research and in the subsequent theoretical interpretations lies in exactly what is being studied. The two studies cited above compare and contrast various conditions, each of which can lead to cognitive changes at the behavioural level. Which condition best facilitates or benefits learning depends on these same various factors and how they are combined for study. So Kruger (1993) paired eight-year-old girls with a peer (in this case, their best friend) or with their mother for discussion of moral dilemmas. In contrast, Druyan (2001) paired children at pre-school, in Grade 3 and in Grade 5 with either peers or adults, and she included either social or tactile conditions for each pairing. Both studies are thus multivariate in nature and consider a range of variables within and between children. It is hard to find the common ground in the two studies, and indeed a quick glance at the references cited reveals very little overlap in those studies considered influential in the development of the research questions, the results and their interpretation. In such circumstances, it may not be so surprising that two quite different and broad theoretical interpretations may be applicable.

One solution to this confusion may be to start by looking at peer collaboration. A useful edited volume was published in 1999 examining peer learning (O'Donnell & King, 1999), in which two separate chapters deal with the implications of Piagetian and Vygotskian theory for peer learning (De Lisi & Golbeck, 1999; Hogan & Tudge, 1999, respectively). The literature reviewed thus falls separately into two theoretical frameworks while the focus is on peer learning (the actual term used fluctuates, often as a consequence of the theoretical emphasis but sometimes because of the research question). However, what is important is that the focus is on peers – that is, children regarded as equals, however defined, but usually of similar age, social status and educational level.

In a section of their chapter concerned with the implications of Piagetian theory for peer learning, De Lisi and Golbeck (1999) start with an overview of Piaget's work on moral reasoning in children, which, as noted in Chapter 2, underpins much of the subsequent research on peer interaction and the role of children's discussions in promoting cognitive growth. Some of this work, including that of Kruger (1992, 1993) for example, was reviewed in Chapter 2. As well as studying children's social reasoning, they also examine logical reasoning, claiming that this illustrates the breadth of Piaget's theory. Both types of reasoning lend themselves to the study of the role of peer interaction. It has already been noted that Piaget's theory is generally characterised as underplaying the role that any form of socialisation plays in children's cognitive development; however, the role that cooperation between peers plays in socialisation was also discussed. De Lisi and Golbeck summarise the work of Kruger by noting that peer interaction enhances moral reasoning, that the discussions between peers are qualitatively different from those between children and adults, and that the use of active reasoning, characteristic of peer pairs, is predictive of more sophisticated individual reasoning post-test. Active reasoning was determined by the relative contribution made and engagement by the children as they worked together. Higher levels of active engagement were noted in peer pairs.

So, in studies of moral reasoning, in the Piagetian tradition, peer interaction, emphasising as it does social equality, leads to cognitive development through the provision of a social situation that promotes active
discussion by participants. Specifically, communication with a peer in an
egalitarian way facilitates higher levels of moral reasoning in eight-year-
old girls.

An examination of how peer interaction can facilitate scientific reasoning draws attention to how social interaction can contribute to cognitive change (enhanced scientific reasoning) in young children. The research
was mainly conducted in the 1970s and 1980s (reviewed in Garton, 1992),
and much of the work was directed at identifying those conditions that
did (and did not) lead to improvement in children's reasoning. Theoretical explanations for the improvements took various forms, including social
learning, modelling (active and passive), co-operation and conflict. The
theoretical explanations vary depending on the particular combinations or
groupings of children, the extent of their involvement with the materials
and/or the other participants, and the comparison groups. The one thread
in common is that, in general, Piagetian tasks were used, typically a conservation task. Furthermore, frequently a non-conserving child was the
focal child and was paired with a child who had previously demonstrated
success on the particular task. Success was typically measured by demonstrated post-test improvement in the less able child coupled with explanations that support the solution and that are novel to the child, hence
showing an understanding of the principles learned through interaction.
Variously, the phrase 'socio-cognitive conflict' is used to encapsulate what
it is about the peer interaction that facilitates such cognitive change. The
phrase has its origins in Piagetian theory but includes the social element
as a contributory factor. As defined in Chapter 1, cognitive conflict was
regarded as the trigger for changes in the ways in which internalised representations of actions were organised. Socio-cognitive conflict acknowledges that such changes can be triggered by social factors as well as
biological ones.

Levin and Druyan (1993) examine where socio-cognitive conflict fails,
noting (as we have also noted here) that, in a Piagetian framework, one
important constraint is the child's age. Children who have not reached the
operational stage cannot benefit from interaction, since they are incapable
of the decentring required to benefit from opposing views expressed during
interaction. Furthermore, they argue, the cognitive distance or discrepancy
in knowledge between the two children may be a further limitation, with
children benefiting most from interacting with children whose ability is in
advance of their own. In addition, passive participation (as opposed to
active engagement) in the interaction does not generally lead to any mea-

surable benefit to the individual child. Levin and Druyan further comment on Tudge's (1992) observations that, under some circumstances, some children actually regress after social interaction. Regression can be accommodated within a Vygotskian interpretation of the value of social interaction. Direction of change at post-test was predicted by children's level of confidence. Such a finding prompted Levin and Druyan to ask whether there may be tasks that evoke scientific misconceptions and resist development improvement, which may be 'regression-inducing'. Such misconceptions are defined as those incompatible with scientific knowledge and as being resistant to change through education and experience. An example (and the one used by Levin and Druyan) is the misconception that a single object moves in its entirety in a single motion, and hence all parts of the object move at the same speed (an example is a rotating car tyre).

Using tasks that may be resistant to cognitive change and those that potentially facilitate cognitive development, Levin and Druyan (1993) compared both intrapersonal and interpersonal conflict. They point out that they are not pitting a Piagetian position against a Vygotskian one, since both mention a role for social interaction; rather the interest lies in the role of the two forms of conflict. Intrapersonal conflict was induced by providing children with conflicting judgements, while interpersonal conflict was generated by the formation of transaction groups of two boys and two girls who were instructed to discuss and arrive at a consensual answer to the various problems. Using the misconception described above, two problems were used: an autonomous motion problem, whereby two dogs were running in concentric circles, with one circle noticeably larger than the other, and a common carrier problem, in which the two dogs were linked and moved on a rotating carousel. In the former, the dogs' legs moved to indicate independent motion, while in the latter, they were immobile. The autonomous motion variation is considered to be development-prone in that schooling and/or age will lead to the right answer (in terms of estimating linear speed). The common carrier problem is regarded as development-resistant, since children are likely to 'hang onto' the incorrect response. It was predicted that working on the former problem would lead to children advancing cognitively while, after working on the latter, they would demonstrate regression.

The children who participated in this study are older than those on whom I have tended to focus so far, ranging from 11 to 15 years. Approximately half of the participants were boys. A pre-test/interaction/post-test design was used, with an immediate post-test and a delayed post-test, some two to three months later. Various interventions were compared: group intervention, individual multiple-choices, and no intervention. The analyses are comprehensive and reasonably complex, and for our purposes it is sufficient to focus on the conclusions, since it is here that theoretical implications are discussed. In support of the predictions, children generally progressed cognitively after exposure to the autonomous motion/development-prone task and regressed after intervention with the common carrier/development-resistant task. In the latter, they continued to prefer the misconception over the scientific explanation. In addition, peer interaction facilitated improvements in the development-prone condition and had a mixed effect (both progress and regression) in the development-resistant condition. Levin and Druyan note that interpersonal interaction, given certain circumstances – in this case, development-prone problems – can provoke conflict. They also comment, however, that any outcome is not related directly to the intensity of the conflict. By contrast, cognitive change was related to intrapersonal conflict in both types of problem. Greater conflict between peers generates intrapersonal conflict, which in turn can induce cognitive change, but only on the development-resistant problems, and that change was regressive. The researchers claim that this mixed result seriously questions a strong Piagetian position that posits an overarching role for conflict and disequilibrium as the instigator of cognitive development.

A Vygotskian framework, however, can explain the regression by speculating that, during social exchanges and discussion, children come to adopt social and cultural values and concepts. A misconception can be regarded as a cultural artifact, generated and perpetuated by the community, and as such, Levin and Druyan argue, social interaction is in fact an efficient way for the child to learn current community values and knowledge even in an esoteric domain such as problem solving.

An interesting aspect discussed by Levin and Druyan is the distinction between development-prone problems and development-resistant problems and how they relate to the development of knowledge in children. The finding that younger children perform better on the former problems, while all ages (including adults) perform similarly on the latter, is empirical. The distinction does not dwell on the psychological consequences of actually having the incorrect answer to the latter type of problem. Again, like Tudge (1992), the notion of confidence is invoked to account for successful performance on the development-prone tasks (where the correct answer was obtained) and for improved post-test performance.

In summary, the changes noted from pre-test to post-test in these young people were related to the types of task and the nature of the conflict during the interaction. The more strongly a view was held during interaction, the higher was the probability of such a response being demonstrated during individual post-test. This is true for both progression and regression, although, as is pointed out, it is not clear which causal mechanisms are at work in one, other or both cases. What this study does is highlight the complexities involved in interpreting the results of social problem solving tasks. Again, the issues are the nature of the problem under investigation, the nature of the interaction, as well as the ages of children involved and the nature of the social groupings involved. As noted earlier, every study published adopts a particular theoretical and/or empirical paradigm, depending on the particular research question(s). But such variations between studies make it very difficult to generalise the findings and to provide interpretations consistent with the different theoretical frameworks. The Levin and Druyan (1993) study finds that both a Piagetian conflict solution and a Vygotskian social framework can explain certain findings. But no single model in this case can incorporate all the elements or all the results, which again points to the complexities of research that examines the role of peer interaction on children's cognitive development. There is no single experimental paradigm, no single definition of what constitutes a problem for children (and the related problem of there then being no single definition of a solution – either the process or the outcome) and no unitary theoretical explanation that can comprehensively enable description and prediction of children's cognitive development.

The bulk of the evidence described here and elsewhere supports a position that a Piagetian view can be used to interpret various forms of interaction (usually of a conflictual nature) and where moral and scientific reasoning is involved. Deviations in results (i.e., inconsistent with a Piagetian socio-cognitive conflict interpretation) are generally found to be consistent or compatible with some aspect of Vygotsky's social theory. From a Vygotskian perspective, the nature of the problem solving task *per se* is not so important – that is, it would not necessarily be derived from the theory itself. But the profile of the peer pair, dyad or group must be interpretable with the ZPD – in other words, there must be some knowledge differential between participants. Consequently, most studies use an idiosyncratic combination of variables, not necessarily to compare and contrast the theories, but to enable objective measurement of cognitive change, usually in the less able, less knowledgeable participant.

PEER INTERACTION IN THE CLASSROOM

De Lisi and Golbeck (1999) also discuss classroom research, which has tended to be neglected in mainstream developmental psychological research, looking at the influence of peer interaction on cognitive outcomes and learning. De Lisi and Golbeck only focused on the work of one research team (headed by DeVries), which has extensively studied the role of peer interaction in the development of social reasoning, specifically the construction of social knowledge, in the classroom. DeVries and Goncu (1987, cited in De Lisi & Golbeck, 1999), for example, examined the extent to which classrooms that encourage co-operation lead children to demonstrate higher levels of interpersonal negotiation strategies. They compared two different education programs, each providing their four-year-old children with different interaction experiences as part of their curricula. The classroom environment, including teachers' didactic styles, was described and related to the children's behaviour in relation to their interpersonal understanding.

This work has spawned research examining how the classroom environment influences children's interpersonal and socio-moral understanding. Constructivist classrooms, which focus on reasoning, allow children greater freedom to make their own choices and to work reciprocally with teachers. It is believed that such an atmosphere promotes greater interpersonal awareness and enables children to develop their own classroom rules (Castles & Rogers, 1993) and engage in the democratic process. They have greater ownership of their behaviour and display higher levels of sensitivity towards others, respect for one another and maintenance of friendships and other close relationships. A constructivist classroom, unlike one that is teacher-led, creates a community spirit where active involvement in encouraged. This type of environment has subsequent benefits for children and their social and moral behaviours.

Rogoff (1998) discusses how peers may be able to assist one another in the classroom, and uses the examples of peer tutoring and peer collaboration, each of which has been shown to be effective for both the learner and the tutor. I will confine my examination of Rogoff's discussion to the role that school classrooms can play in providing opportunities for peer interaction and children's learning. Elsewhere I touch on the processes by which collaboration can be established and fostered, as well as research that shows the cognitive benefits deriving from peer interaction. Rogoff reminds her reader that, in schools, students are generally taught by adult teachers, but, and perhaps more importantly, in any study or use of peer collaboration, there is a 'hidden' adult. In research studies there are often experimenters lurking in the background, and in classrooms there are teachers. While the part social status or role might play in various forms of collaboration has not received the research attention it warrants (with the exception of Rogoff's discussion), it is obvious that adults play a role, even if covert, in designing situations that hopefully maximise efforts at peer collaboration.

Rogoff calls upon educators to think about the role(s) adults play when encouraging peer collaboration in the classroom, as well as practical issues like the layout or structure of the classroom. Teachers need to understand not only the teaching/learning principles underpinning collaborative learning, but also some of the more subtle aspects of their role and contribution to the process. Rogoff draws attention to educational programs that help 'teachers learn how to help children learn how to support each other's work in the classroom through co-operation' (Rogoff, 1998, p. 721). Ultimately, and this is a view that is tacitly endorsed in this chapter, if not the whole book, the encouragement of shared thinking between children requires, at some level, adult assistance or input. This assistance in turn reflects the social and cultural context in which the learning is taking place, including institutions such as schools. Again, this view is contrasted with a social influence position, whereby two children are placed in a situation in which they are expected to work together. The broader context must be included to be able to describe how children learn to co-operate, collaborate and communicate to facilitate learning.

PEER INTERACTION AND ADULT–CHILD INTERACTION

It was noted previously that peer interaction, either of dyads or groups, has tended to characterise research interpreted or explained by a Piagetian or socio-cognitive conflict framework. Relevant experimental comparisons are usually made between different aged children, different forms of intervention/interaction, children of different abilities and the use of different reasoning-type problems. Interpersonal conflict is largely regarded as the mechanism by which individual cognitive change is triggered, though how it actually works and why it causes progression under most circumstances has not been explained.

Hogan and Tudge (1999) consider the implications of Vygotsky's theory for peer learning. They acknowledge that they need to adopt a broad view of the theory and not simply focus on the ZPD for a description of what happens when peers or a child and adult work together to solve problems. They further acknowledge that most of the research inspired directly by Vygotsky's theory involves adult–child pairs. However, it must be remembered that Vygotsky's theory is frequently invoked when a Piagetian explanation is not applicable in peer interaction studies. By and large, the optimal conditions under which children can benefit from working with a peer or a more capable adult have been shown to be variable and the benefits of social interaction in terms of improved cognitive or problem solving capacity ambiguous. Furthermore, how the interaction specifically facilitates cognitive change in the less capable or less knowledgeable partner is not clear. Among possible contenders, communication has been mentioned (Garton, 1992), as have specific types of communication (e.g., Garton & Pratt, 2001; Garton, Harvey & Pratt, submitted; Teasley, 1995), the role the more capable partner plays in regulating the joint problem solving (e.g., Wertsch et al., 1980), and the initial absolute and relative levels of competence and the distance or discrepancy between these at the start of the interaction. Hogan and Tudge also list 'the age and ability level of the children and of their partner, the children's motivation to collaborate, and the extent to which they are exposed to more sophisticated reasoning by a partner and are willing to accept and use that reasoning independently. The nature of the task will also have an influence' (Hogan & Tudge, 1999, p. 46). Thus, individual, interpersonal and cultural factors are all regarded not only as cornerstones of Vygotsky's theory, but as matters that need to inform any theoretical account of the role of social interaction in the facilitation of problem solving and in benefiting cognitive change.

Individual factors include age and gender, according to Hogan and Tudge. I will later argue that there are other individual factors, including relative and/or absolute ability or competence level, readiness to participate in, contribute to or benefit from collaborative problem solving, and a sensitivity towards the partner that can have a profound influence on the extent to which learning can and does occur. Interpersonal factors are 'processes taking place between individuals' (Hogan & Tudge, 1999, p, 48), which include the nature of the collaborative pairing (peer or adult–child), ability differentials between partners, and affective, emotional factors, including relative confidence of partners and the goals aspired to by partners, levels of joint understanding, interaction style and the role of feedback. In particular, I shall return to affective factors and the issue of joint understanding and awareness later in this chapter.

There are several other ways in which the social interaction between two people solving a problem can be characterised theoretically. As before, most of these have direct or indirect links with Piagetian or Vygotskian theories, or modern variations thereof. I will describe briefly how each area has contributed to the theorising around the descriptions and predictions of cognitive change during and after collaborative problem solving.

THEORY OF MIND AND PROBLEM SOLVING

Theory of mind can be characterised as social cognitive knowledge – that is, knowledge of people, specifically their mental states. Theory of mind as a field of study encompasses research that examines how people make sense of their worlds, of themselves, of others, of interpersonal relations – social and cognitive processes that are apparent in everyday life. Theory of mind explanations and empirical studies have burgeoned over the past 20 years, and many researchers have adopted a theory of mind framework for their work. Theory of mind as a lay concept has been characterised as folk psychology, which is a commonsense approach to human psychology and accords a central role to beliefs, desires and thoughts both in the self and in others. Much of the minutiae need not concern us here, since the theory has not proved widely applicable in collaborative problem solving. The main questions are:

- Is theory of mind a theory? That is, can it explain and predict behaviour?
- Is it falsifiable?
- What is the nature (content and structure) of the adult theory of mind?
- Furthermore, from a developmental perspective, how does theory of mind develop?

There has been considerable debate in the developmental psychology literature on these topics, and various characterisations of children's development (how, when, conditions for application) have been put forward. For the purposes of this book, the relevance of theory of mind research for cognitive development lies in how a child's theory of human mental processes can be developed and applied in different domains, which can include problem solving.

Carpendale and Lewis (in press) argue for theory of mind developing in a triadic relationship between the child, others and the environment. Children interact with the world and also communicate with others about their understanding and beliefs. This theory draws on both Piaget and Vygotsky and is consistent with the view that the social interaction component is critical to children's cognitive development. Carpendale and Lewis see an application of a variant of this perspective for the development of children's social understanding and theory of mind. In other words, children's theory of mind develops through social interaction, by which an understanding of thoughts and beliefs is constructed. Carpendale and Lewis cite a body of research literature to support their position, touching on studies of reasoning. They contend that children understand talk about psychological states through the patterns of interaction for which those words are used. So by using language about the social, emotional and psychological world, in appropriate contexts, children can begin to think about how others are thinking and feeling. Social processes underpin infants' dyadic interaction and shared meaning through to false belief understanding and complex social skills.

Flavell and Miller (1998) cite three reasons why theory of mind is important for social cognitive development and for the application of an integrated theory by the developing child:

1. It integrates social cognitive development with other areas of development. Theory of mind is applied to diverse areas, such as domain-specific knowledge development and emotional development.
2. It integrates social cognitive development with other areas, such as neurophysiology, cognitive science and philosophy.
3. The new focus on the development of the content and structure of mind has enabled the posing of questions regarding how and when children acquire an understanding of beliefs, thoughts and desires, and the relationship of these understandings with developments in other behaviours.

Theory of mind regards the child as developing increasingly sophisticated and complex representational systems in an attempt to understand others. It is not generally applied to cognitive development, let alone problem solving, although it has been linked to improvements noted after collaborative problem solving. This is because, it is argued, an awareness of the other in interaction and in collaboration, specifically awareness of the other as a source of knowledge, can facilitate problem solving. Flavell and Miller (1998) discuss some major implications of theory of mind for the realm of social cognition with which collaborative problem solving has links. Relevant topics include children's understanding of mental states such as thinking and knowledge. These mental states are used to explain and predict behaviour, both of the self and of others, and are part of an integrated system linking mind and behaviour. It is important in the context of collaborative problem solving that children are aware of and able to use the mental states of the other participant in the collaboration. They need to be aware of the knowledge state of the other person and that such knowledge may or may not be the same as their own. Being explicitly aware of such differences would lead to greater proficiency in problem solving as children would know what the starting knowledge is and how that can be used, or changed, to facilitate a solution to a particular problem. Making explicit such knowledge is regarded as a vital step in successful collaboration. But in order to make it explicit, children have to be aware that differences may exist, which requires them to have a theory about others as well as themselves.

Theory of mind as an explanation of how social process can assist learning or cognitive change can have particular value in cases where a child is paired with a more capable peer or adult who can be regarded as the expert. Communication between participants can establish levels of knowledge, and the way in which more advanced knowledge can be tapped and used is the medium through which transfer of knowledge can take place. Research has been looking at the language used in interaction to try to identify what sorts of exchanges facilitate learning in less able children (Garton & Harvey, submitted; Garton, Harvey, & Pratt, submitted; Garton & Pratt, 2001; O'Connor, 2000). But there has been no research into how children talk to one another to establish levels of knowledge and expertise or to sort out roles and responsibilities *before* they begin the task.

The work by Garton and colleagues focuses on the communicative aspects of interaction between peers or between children and adults. The general aim was twofold:

1. to describe the communication patterns during problem solving and to link these to subsequent independent problem solving; and
2. to see if the language used showed that the children were aware that the partner had a similar or different knowledge status and, if the partner were more knowledgeable, how this could be accessed or used to benefit learning.

Garton and Pratt (2001) conducted a study based on the assumption that cognitive processes would be reflected by various communicative tasks such as planning, monitoring, sharing of knowledge and task regulation. It was proposed that analysis of the language used by a dyad would provide a window into the process of collaboration. In addition, using two different but related tasks for the collaboration and pre-/post-test phases permitted evaluation of whether general or task-specific problem solving strategies were developed and communicated during the collaborative process. The study aimed to make pre- to post-test comparisons of the problem solving behaviour of children in the various dyads.

In accordance with the theoretical framework offered by Vygotsky's ZPD, the target child in the experimental condition was always working with a more capable peer, as determined at pre-testing. Comparison was provided through contrast pairs of children of similar ability and control children who did not engage in collaboration.

The research revealed that lower ability children of four and seven years of age, when paired with same-aged children of relatively higher ability, showed improved performance after interaction when compared to same-ability pairs or children who did not engage in collaboration. Differences in language use were also found, with seven-year-old children using more procedural and descriptive language than younger children when interacting with their partner. In addition, lower ability children (of both ages) used 'checking' language more frequently, suggesting they were aware at some level of the knowledge or skill discrepancy between them and their partner. Despite these findings, enhanced problem solving performance could not be linked to the specific patterns of language used by either partner in the interaction.

SELF-REGULATION IN PROBLEM SOLVING

According to Vygotsky's theory, one of the main challenges for children is the ability to take on responsibility for solving a problem. This is usually viewed as children developing the capacity to self-regulate, adopting the roles and responsibilities of the more expert partner, in the ZPD. Many studies have looked at how parental regulation (verbal and non-verbal) can influence children's problem solving as well as their capacity for self-regulation. These forms of regulation include taking responsibility for the various components of the task (their sequential organisation and their completion, for example) and behaviours such as pointing, directing attention and monitoring, which assist in solving the problem. Such behaviours are initially restricted to the adult, who ensures his or her behaviours are in advance of the child's, and are then transferred to the child during the course of the joint problem solving task. This is not instruction but is better characterised as 'teaching/learning', as the parental behaviour ('teaching') is predictive of the child's subsequent independent problem solving performance, which is better than that displayed before the interaction (hence, 'learning').

Wertsch, McNamee, McLane and Budwig (1980), in one of the first studies on the benefits of maternal regulation of young children's problem solving, investigated how social group processes contributed to a theoretical understanding of how children become independent 'cognitive agent(s)'. Eighteen mother–child dyads took part in the study: six dyads of children with average age two years nine months, six with average age three years seven months, and six with average age of four years five months. The pairs worked together to complete a puzzle in accordance with a model. Some of the puzzle pieces could only be correctly inserted after consultation with the model. As well as examining success in placing the puzzle pieces correctly, child and maternal verbal and non-verbal behaviours were coded – specifically, the child's gazes to the materials involved in the problem, the mother's and child's points to objects or locations, and the handling of the puzzle pieces by both partners. The main interest lay in the extent to which the children consulted the model through gazes as a guide to correct puzzle piece placement, and the behaviours immediately before and after the consultation.

The researchers found that while there was no age difference in the number of gazes recorded, there was a decrease with age in the number of child gazes that were regulated by the mother. This was taken as evidence of increasing self-regulation with age. Furthermore, in general, it was found that when children consulted the model (whether on their own initiative or after maternal gaze or point), younger children were often unable to use that knowledge to insert the appropriate puzzle piece, but older children were able to make independent use of the information. As well as the ontogenetic development from other-regulation to self-regulation, change *within* the interaction (or microgenetic change) was analysed. In this case, while there were individual examples of a shift within a session, the overall data did not suggest that shifts occurred at the microgenetic level. The researchers concluded that the older children were able to understand the strategic utility of maternal regulation not only to insert puzzle pieces successfully but also to take over the responsibility for solving the problem and acting independently. This was further supported by the results that showed mothers providing younger children with greater assistance through verbal and non-verbal means. The trailblazing study was regarded as providing clear support for the Vygotskian shift from interpersonal regulation to intrapersonal regulation in the ZPD.

Freund (1990) argues that much of the research conducted in the same vein as Wertsch et al.'s confounds child competence with child age and does not measure children's independent performance, or mastery, after interaction. She further claims that this failure to measure performance means that it is impossible to determine whether the adult regulation is appropriate or whether differences in regulation are a function of age differences, competence differences or other differences, such as language level or adult expectations. She cites evidence to suggest that 'task regulation is indeed related more to age-related expectations of task difficulty than actual child competence' (Freund, 1990, p. 114).

However, research prior to 1990 that had looked for changes in adult regulation as a function of child competence within an adult–child pair had been inconclusive in disentangling the effects of age and competence. At a more general level, Freund (1990) commented that none of the research on joint adult–child problem solving had been designed to demonstrate any improvements in the individual performance of the children. In order to rectify this, Freund proposed to study the effect that the mother–child interaction had on subsequent independent child performance and the variability in the regulatory behaviours of the mothers as a function of child age, task difficulty and task component. In addition, the independent performance of three- and five-year-old children after interaction with their mothers was compared with the performance of children who had received corrective feedback from the adult experimenter. This was deemed necessary to validate the role of maternal regulation as opposed to mere correction.

A sorting task was used, with easy and difficult versions, and hypotheses developed predicting outcomes depending on task difficulty, age of child and competence of the child. Briefly, in the interaction sessions, mothers were instructed to sort the task materials (miniature furniture grouped into rooms as for a typical house) and to assist, not teach, their children in whatever way they felt comfortable. Both levels of difficulty were completed, counterbalanced across children. Children also completed a familiarisation pre-test sorting task with similar materials and then completed the task independently with different items.

Children's performance on each sorting presentation was calculated from the accuracy of the groupings of furniture based on adult groupings of functional relationships between furniture items, using an algorithm that took into account the number of items, the number of rooms and the number of non-furniture distractor items not grouped. The mother's activities (the task components) during the joint interaction session were coded as: item selection; selection of an appropriate room; and placement of the item in the room. The mother could either take responsibility for a component of the task if she undertook the action or regulate the child's performance if she hinted or directed the child's actions. A component could also be self-regulated if the child selected an item, a room or placed an item without any guidance from his or her mother. Frequencies for these activities were calculated. Maternal verbal content was also coded and analysed; the categories used were: reference to task-specific materials (such as labelling items); strategies for item or room selection; plans, goals and monitoring (such as 'let's do such and such'); and 'other', including feedback and commentary.

The results indicated that aspects of the interaction between mothers and their young children do have an influence on improved independent problem solving in the children. Specifically, children who engaged in social interaction as opposed to receiving feedback only subsequently made more correct ('adult-like') groupings of the materials. This suggests that it is the social interaction element and not just the correct answer that is the key to improved performance by children. Freund also indicated that improved performance was likely to be further enhanced for participants who already had a high level of shared understanding and common knowledge working on a task, albeit a difficult one, which used familiar material, namely furniture. This notion that mothers (and others who have spent considerable periods of time with the child) are in a privileged position with respect to being able to guide and monitor their child's behaviour, with subsequent advantages to the child's cognitive development, is an important one. It has, however, not received the attention it ought in the discussions of the role of social interaction and how the partner's social status, relationship with the child or level of expertise can be hugely influential on facilitating children's problem solving.

Regulation of the child by the mother was most marked in the difficult version of the task, and examples where she took responsibility were also noted in this condition. As the task became easier, the mother's role tended to be more regulatory and more general, enabling children to take increasing responsibility themselves in conditions where the task was less demanding. Further maternal responsibility and regulation were affected by the age of the children, with mothers of three-year-olds taking greater responsibility for the critical component of the task (room selection) while mothers of five-year-olds used more planning and monitoring language. This finding, however, can be linked to children's language competence or familiarity with problem-solving-type tasks, themselves age-related, but also potential confounds. In general, the level of regulation was related to age, which in turn was assumed to be related to competence. Overall, the 'best scenario' was where there was improvement in children's independent problem solving as a consequence of mothers varying the way they regulated their children's behaviour 'in a manner consistent with task demands and (they) offered more strategy, planning, goal directing, and monitoring content in their verbalizations' (Freund, 1990, p. 125). This, it is argued, supports Vygotsky's theory, as well as dealing with methodological shortcomings identified in previous studies.

HELP SEEKING IN PROBLEM SOLVING

Puustinen (1998) discusses the development of self-regulation in children's help-seeking behaviour. The ability to know when and how to seek help is an important development. Children need to be able to tell when they do not know something, to know whom they may go for the information they need, and have the capacity to approach that person and ask relevant and appropriate questions. This is a complex behaviour with several components and, not surprisingly, has been studied in various guises. The work of Nelson-Le Gall and colleagues (e.g., Nelson-Le Gall, 1985; Nelson-Le Gall, DeCooke & Jones, 1989; Nelson-Le Gall, Kratzer, Jones & DeCooke, 1990) examines the social and cognitive aspects associated with help-seeking. Acknowledging the complexity of the behaviour, she characterises help-seeking as comprising five components: awareness of the need for help, deciding to seek help, identifying potential helper(s), using strategies to elicit help, and reactions to help-seeking efforts.

Help-seeking behaviour has theoretical links to theory of mind (awareness that others have knowledge that can be useful) and to Vygotsky's theory. Winnykamen (1992, 1993, cited in Puustinen, 1998) has been credited with situating help-seeking in a framework that examines interactive knowledge acquisition. Help-seeking is thus regarded as interactive and also involves a shift from other-regulation to self-regulation. The ZPD can help to explain children's help-seeking behaviour in collaborative problem solving. Children realise they cannot solve a problem alone so they request assistance (from the adult or more competent peer, which begs the question of how a child can gauge or ascertain the level of competence of a peer). In this way, they demonstrate awareness that, with expert assistance, they will be able to solve the particular problem successfully. Clearly, this is a different interpretation about what happens in interactions during problem solving from that construed in a Vygotskian framework. Generally, the more expert partner is regarded as being the initiator of the actions that lead to a transfer of responsibility for solving the problem to the novice or the less competent child. In the help-seeking interpretation, the child is accorded a more active role in being aware of the need for help and requesting or seeking it and then using that new knowledge to complete the task or solve the problem.

Puustinen's (1998) own research study was conducted against this sort of background. She aimed to look at the development of self-regulation in help-seeking behaviour, using a Vygotskian theoretical framework. In the first instance, she operationalised self-regulation as:

- the awareness of the need for help;
- the restriction of questions to those necessary; and
- reinvestment of help already received.

She developed these from a review of existing literature on help-seeking, transfer and generalisability of information, and reinvestment of help, and from talking to teachers of young children about children's use of questions.

In the study, Puustinen (1998) compared seven- and ten-year old children, the latter being referred to, somewhat ambiguously, as 'advanced'. Children solved logical reasoning problems, independently, with the opportunity to seek help, if they thought it necessary, from the experimenter, who would provide them with an explanation that would assist them to solve the problem (instrumental help) or with the solution (executive help).

It was hypothesised that the older children would be more aware of the need to ask for help, and would be better able to restrict their help-seeking behaviours and to re-use previous explanations received for other similar tasks. As well as recording the actual behaviours, the children provided a self-evaluation score on a 10-point scale.

Awareness of the need to seek help was measured by examining the fit between performance on the reasoning tasks and the score on the self-evaluation scale. Six help-seeking behaviours were identified from the videotape transcriptions. These were used to examine what types of questions were asked, including confirmatory comments. Reinvestment of received help was obtained from the absence of other help-seeking behaviours in the presence of questions. This was taken as indication of an understanding of the solution and was regarded as evidence for self-regulation.

While the age-related changes in behaviours were not as marked as had been expected, older children and academically high achievers were able to show greater self-regulation of their help-seeking behaviour. Academic achievement was, in fact, a better predictor of self-regulation in all three areas under investigation – namely, awareness of the need to obtain help, restriction of the questions and reinvestment of strategies or knowledge. High-achieving older children conformed in all respects to the strict definition of a self-regulated help-seeker.

The results of this research have implications for the study of collaborative problem solving where, instead of the experimenter, the child is working jointly with another person, be it an adult or a peer of lesser, similar or greater ability. In Puustinen's (1998) work, the role of experimenter is confounded with social status. Children who have attended school will be used to asking questions of the teacher as a way of seeking help. It would be interesting to see what happens in collaborative problem solving where the major issue, certainly in peer interaction, is to establish the knowledge status of the partner. Having made some decision about whether the partner is a likely source of knowledge or help, then there is the associated issue of the less able partner being aware of not having the relevant expertise. This ties in very closely with the theory of mind perspective on children's cognitive development and would be worth exploring in greater depth in the future.

THE ROLE OF TALK IN COLLABORATIVE PROBLEM SOLVING

One way of looking at how children's problem solving can improve after interacting with an adult or a more capable peer is to examine the nature of the interaction itself. In some ways, the earlier studies of Wertsch and colleagues and of Freund, discussed earlier in the chapter, started to identify aspects of the interaction that may be beneficial to learning. Those earlier studies looked at verbal and nonverbal aspects of the regulatory role played, in these cases, by the mother and examined how these aspects, and their transfer to the child, assisted in the subsequent improvements in the child's problem solving ability. But what happens when two children are paired to work together? This was the question picked up by Teasley (1995). She draws on previous work that considered peer collaboration and that emphasised the role of communication in interaction (see also Garton, 1993). She summarises the research to date on both the development and role of private speech (as described in both Piagetian and Vygotskian research) and think-aloud speech – that is, concurrent verbalisation – during problem solving. She concludes that both sets of research highlight the close relationship between problem solving and talking, and the gains that can be attributed to the role of speech. Similar sorts of speech, such as arguments, clarification and explanation, are also noted in the communication in collaborative problem solving and can contribute to the apparent success of such interactions.

In order to study the relationship between talk and problem solving, Teasley (1995) determined that it was necessary to separate the two variables. To do this, she added additional experimental groups to the traditional peer collaboration pairings – namely, children who work alone and talk aloud and children with partners who are not allowed to talk. The specific research hypotheses were:

- Children who talk would solve problems more effectively than those who did not talk.
- Talk that is interpretive (plans, strategies) would be associated with greater learning than no talk or irrelevant talk.
- Children who worked with peers would produce more talk, and more interpretive talk, than children who worked alone.

The task was a scientific reasoning one, and the children were aged around ten years. Children participated in a pre-test training session, a session where they either worked alone or in same-sex pairs and were instructed to talk or not to talk, and a post-test interview. Interest was therefore in the capacity of the children to solve the reasoning tasks in the intervention phase and not in any subsequent learning.

Both the amount of talk (number of utterances) and the type of talk (coded in categories) were analysed, and the reasoning tasks were scored according to a number of dimensions, including number of hypotheses generated. These hypotheses varied in complexity but yielded quantitative data at the level of the individual child, which were used for comparison purposes. In summary, the results showed that children in talk dyads generated better hypotheses to the solution of the problem (though not always significantly so) than the no-talk children who worked either alone or in dyads. Furthermore, children in talk dyads had a significantly better understanding of the solution than no-talk children who worked alone. In general, however, the talk/no-talk variable was of greater importance than the dyad/individual variable in so far as talking contributed to a greater extent to eventual success. But some of the talk was social and some was self-directed, and Teasley (1995) wished to unpack this distinction through comparison of the amount and type of talk in the two conditions. She recognised that the talk of children who worked alone was characterised by pauses and variability in the overall amount. Having a partner ensured that communication was ongoing and fluid, but it would be naïve to conclude that more talk *per se* led to better performance. There were also qualitative differences in the type of talk: children in dyads produced more interpretive or strategic talk, while children who worked alone produced more descriptive talk.

In conclusion, Teasley (1995) demonstrates that 'children who produced talk as they worked with partners on a scientific reasoning task had higher rated final hypotheses than did children – with partners or alone – who did not talk' (p. 217). In other words, the study shows the benefits to successful problem solving of talk, especially when working with a partner. This seems to enhance the opportunity to develop hypotheses that enable the solution of reasoning problems. There are some qualifications added to Teasley's general conclusions, but she finishes by discussing the implications of the cognitive benefits of joint talk for classroom learning and instruction.

Garton, Harvey and Pratt (submitted) investigated language use in and outcomes of parent–child problem solving dyads, as well as comparing these with outcomes from child–child dyads reported previously (Garton & Pratt, 2001). This study paid particular attention to the language used in the interactions between individual children and their parents. The children were aged around four years and participated in an individual pre- and post-test as well as an interaction session with their parent. It was expected that children would benefit cognitively from collaborating with an adult, in terms of improved performance on a related sorting task. It was also predicted that the primary mechanism of cognitive change (as measured by pre- to post-test improvement) would be the adult assistance in the development of a general strategic approach to sorting tasks reflected in their use of planning language. Finally, it was predicted that the communication patterns of the parent–child dyad would differ from those of peer interactions. In particular, adults may scaffold their child by using checking and planning language, and the children's awareness and understanding of the adult's potential contribution may be reflected in their compliance with adult commands and their own use of procedural language.

In general, these results again showed that four-year-old children showed an improved problem solving capacity after collaborating with their parent on a different sorting task. The analysis demonstrates a significant improvement in sorting skills both for children who participated in the parent–child dyad and for the low ability children in the mixed ability group. This suggests that the superior capacity of the adult and the more capable peer, in terms of problem solving, influenced the performance of less skilled collaborators.

This study aimed to take a closer look at collaboration in terms of language use in addition to problem solving outcomes, in order to gain some insight into the mechanisms involved in this process. In general terms, significant differences were found in the amount and types of language used by parents and children within the parent–child dyad, and by both parents and children within this group in comparison to all the peer group. More specifically, parents working with four-year-old children used a greater number of utterances than any other group. The children in the parent–child dyad also used a greater number of utterances than their counterparts paired with peers of any ability.

The greater number of utterances generated by children in the parent–child pairing is of interest given the significant association between the overall amount of language used and improved problem solving outcomes on a related task. Teasley (1995) found a similar pattern, with total number of collaborative utterances significantly associated with improvements in reasoning strategies. It may be that more frequent talk about the problem solving task leads to improved skills and that parents are more competent at eliciting language from their four-year-old children than are peers. There were also specific differences in the types of language used by parents and children within the collaborative process. When differences in the total amount of language used were accounted for, it was found that parents primarily used their language for checking and commanding their child during the collaboration. The children who worked with adults used more descriptive and procedural language than their parents, and their use of descriptive language was more frequent than any other children. Finally, and most interestingly, there was a relationship between the planning language used by parents and improved problem solving outcomes by the children. This supports the findings of Freund (1990), who demonstrated that parental planning language contributed significantly to improved problem solving outcomes for children.

It was concluded that parental use of language was quite different from high ability children's use of language during the interaction session, despite the same instructions. With one exception (the use of descriptive language), there were no specific differences in the patterns of language used by children, no matter which problem solving group they participated in and despite their initial differences in sorting ability as measured at pre-test. Parental questioning and agreement were used to encourage children to think about the problem solving task in a concrete and purposeful way, as demonstrated by the children's use of procedural and descriptive language. The use of feedback has already been demonstrated to be successful in improving collaboration outcomes (Tudge et al., 1996), and it may be that parents are relatively skilful at determining what type of feedback is required to keep children focused and on task.

The relationship between planning language used by parents and children's improved problem solving at post-test was interpreted by Garton et al. (Garton, Harvey & Pratt, submitted) as supporting a scaffolding explanation for children's cognitive development. Planning language highlights what parents want the child to do, and compliance is then generalised to the related post-test task. The relation of planning language to subsequent child performance also points to the role of children paying attention to, or being aware of, the role of the adult in assisting them during problem solving. In general, it was not simply the rich language environment generated in the parent–child dyad that improved subsequent problem solving. It seems that parents' strategic approach to the collaborative task allowed them to support the child to generate more effective problem solving skills. This is not directly related to expertise at the task, as the more 'expert' or high ability children did not apply the same pattern of language. The results suggest that adult use of specific language functions assist and support the child during learning.

Fawcett and Garton (submitted), using a pre-test/interaction/post-test design, in which children completed sorting tasks, compared two forms of dyadic collaboration – one where the children could talk to one another and one where they were expressly forbidden to talk (which minimised talk but did not eliminate it entirely). A comparison was also made between children who engaged in interaction and children who completed card sorting task alone. The study found that, during the collaborative phase, seven-year-old children working in dyads on a problem solving task achieved significantly more sorts than children working individually. In addition, only those children who were paired with a child of relatively higher ability during the collaborative phase demonstrated improved performance from pre- to post-test. More specifically, the less able children who worked with a more capable peer were subsequently able to complete a relatively greater number of sorts with attribute blocks than children who worked individually, who were paired with a child of similar ability or who worked with a partner of lower ability. This result is identical to that found by Garton and Pratt (2001).

Children who were instructed to talk and provide explanations during the collaborative phase were subsequently able to complete a relatively greater number of sorts of the attribute blocks from pre- to post-test than children in dyads where there was minimal verbal interaction and children who worked independently. This suggests that the active exchange of ideas, rather than merely working together, was integral to improved performance. Further analysis, limited to low sorting ability children collaborating with higher sorting ability peers, showed that children who were required to explain the sort for their partner to perform made significantly greater gains in sorting ability from pre- to post-test than children whose verbal interaction was minimal.

These findings suggest that, although there is a performance benefit for children working collaboratively, the longer-term cognitive benefit for individual children appears to be affected by a number of factors. It seems to be important that children are exposed to a higher level of reasoning than that which they exhibited at pre-test and that they accept this reasoning as valid. In addition, active participation and reasoned communication seem to be critical underlying factors (Fawcett & Garton, submitted).

CONCLUSION

From the research described in this chapter, there are various forms of self-regulation that can be identified and linked with improvements in problem solving and learning. These include the use of verbal and nonverbal means to monitor, discuss and take responsibility for entertaining alternative solutions or hypotheses through a process of intersubjectivity. The preceding studies have used different designs and different ways of studying learning, but each shows that the capacity of young children to adopt, take over or otherwise take advantage of opportunities, however they are presented, to regulate themselves when solving problems, leads to improved problem solving reasoning or learning. In particular, there is added value when children work with a partner or the experiment allows them to seek assistance. It is generally argued that these circumstances encourage co-operation and collaboration, since new ideas are produced, discussed and evaluated, and roles and responsibilities are allocated and negotiated. The extent to which children avail themselves of these opportunities depends, in experimental studies, on the ways in which the study is designed and the theoretical assumptions underpinning the research. It is not sufficient simply to pair children and watch what they do. The situations are carefully crafted, based on a theoretical foundation and robust research questions. Hence the diversity in approaches, although the general conclusions are similar.

Learning, cognitive development or cognitive change is manifested in improved problem solving when a situation is constructed that allows young children to explore options or alternative solutions, to adopt various roles and to learn through co-operation and collaboration. Intersubjectivity is often invoked to describe the mechanism by which the shared thinking and shared responsibility are promoted, which in turn enhance learning. The children learn to think, to master problem solving skills and to develop interpersonal understanding, each of which is necessary for cognitive development (cf. Rogoff, 1998).

CHAPTER 5

WHAT THE CHILD BRINGS TO THE TASK

Most of the research on children's problem solving has been couched in a tradition that aims to describe and predict the average performance of children at certain ages. In the case of collaborative problem solving, children's performance is measured pre-test, post-test and during the interaction, with a focus mainly on any pre- to post-test improvement in average performance, analysed through the use of an ANOVA or similar statistic. My own work has, by contrast, often used a non-parametric measure of improvement in an attempt to gauge relative improvements in performance as well as absolute ones. An individual differences approach would use correlational analyses to look for patterns in the data at all stages of a traditional pre-test/interaction/post-test designed study and between pre- and post-test measures.

Without going into a treatise about the merits of different analytical tools, it is sufficient to note that the measurement and analysis of problem solving performance links in with the debate about what is being measured – cognitive development or cognitive change. This chapter looks at problem solving from an individual perspective and is more closely aligned with the definition of cognitive change in so far as social influences are considered and attributes of the child (social, cognitive, educational) are acknowledged as contributing to individual development and change. Gauvain (2001b) also acknowledges that children contribute in varied ways to the task, and the study of various attributes has extended our understanding of variables that perhaps ought to be considered when looking at interactions that are social but have cognitive consequences.

READINESS TO BENEFIT FROM INTERACTION

Recent research has explored and refined measures of children's readiness to benefit from collaboration. Current expertise or problem solving level, plus cognitive flexibility, is likely to be a more precise predictor of change than problem solving competence level alone. Further, it may be expected that flexibility rather than age *per se* will predict gain. Other characteristics of the children, such as demonstration of existing social awareness, may also play a role, leading to predictions about which children might benefit from social collaboration. This chapter highlights some research into what children bring to problem solving tasks in terms of their knowledge, skills, expertise and capacity to benefit from social interaction and advance cognitively.

COGNITIVE FLEXIBILITY

In recent research, the notion of 'cognitive flexibility' has been invoked as a way of characterising how children approach a problem solving task and the extent to which they examine a problem independently of any previous ones. A child is regarded as 'flexible' if he or she addresses each problem independently of any previous strategy or way of solving the problem presented. In the context of a problem solving task, such flexibility would be demonstrated, for example, by a capacity to understand through correct solutions of a sequence of increasingly complex problems, presented to represent various forms of thinking, that each problem requires independent thinking and conceptualisation. 'Non-flexible' or 'inflexible' children, on the other hand, are characterised by problem solving via algorithm – that is, the adoption of a single strategy or solution, whether correct or incorrect, for all problems. This form of problem solving is further characterised by fast, repetitive responses that seemingly pay little attention to the changing characteristics of problems presented or any awareness of the value of being correct.

Bonino and Cattelino (1999) examined the relationship between 'flexibility in thinking' and the solution of social conflicts with peers. They draw attention to the theoretical positions of Vygotsky and Piaget but point out that most of the research on the relationship between cognitive ability and social behaviour in children has focused on aggression, typically regarded as competitive behaviour. Little work has been conducted examining cognitive abilities and co-operative behaviour. In this research, flexibility was characterised by the ability to suppress a response in order to find a new one – that is, the ability to shift perspective. There are links not only with cognitive theories but with neuropsychology, where the component processes of thinking are described, usually via deficits that appear after brain lesions or injuries. Specifically, Bonino and Cattelino take from clinical research the concept of reactive flexibility, which refers to the capacity to shift responses in reaction to external cues. The task they used was the Wisconsin Card Sorting Task (WCST), often used in neuropsychological testing, which requires participants to inhibit a response that has been previously rewarded for a new, correct one. It is argued that this type of flexibility is important when looking at how partners interact when solving a problem in which they are required to shift their behaviour in response to characteristics of the task.

Seven-year-old children were paired on the basis of gender and flexibility in thinking so that there were girl and boy pairs of high and low flexibility thinkers. Flexibility was determined by individual performance on the WSCT, including the number of correct sorts and the number of persistence errors. In the interaction sessions, co-operative and competitive behaviours were examined through a task that required children to colour in a drawing using pencils that were tied together with a thread. Competitive behaviours were those where both children pulled the thread joining the pencils or where one pulled and the other held the thread tight. Co-operative behaviours were those where one child pulled the thread and the other held it loosely or where no-one pulled the thread because it was offered spontaneously. These interactive modalities were recorded at four crucial times during the colouring-in task. Turn-taking behaviours were also recorded, along with verbal behaviours.

Of interest here are the relationships between cognitive or thinking ability (as measured by flexibility) and performance on the social task that were examined through a series of correlations. The results in general demonstrated that children classified as having a high level of flexibility in their thinking were more able to work co-operatively with their peer, as evidenced by turn taking and not competing for the pencils. They seemed to be avoiding conflict and trying to find novel ways to obtain the pencil for themselves and complete the task. This was interpreted as these high flexibility thinkers suppressing the obvious solution and searching for new solutions. The discussion focuses on the theoretical implications and draws on Field Theory (Lewin, 1951, cited in Bonino & Cattelino, 1999), which does not concern us here. What is important is the conclusion that individual differences in thinking can influence how peers interact and go about solving problems together. It should be noted that the colouring-in task encouraged both co-operation and competition, while most problem solving studies use problems that are neutral and do not force one form of interaction over another. Instead, the interaction emerges through the way the children work together, through their discussion, and negotiation and assessment of the role, responsibilities and abilities of their partner.

Nonetheless, the study by Bonino and Cattelino (1999) fills a void in the literature and provides further evidence that, in studies of collaborative problem solving, it is valuable to take into account aspects other than simple ability level when pairing children. Cognitive flexibility is one type of ability that is related to how children interact and to the subsequent style of the interaction. This could then be important for examining any subsequent benefits for children's thinking after the different types of interaction. The colouring-in task does not permit any study of cognitive benefits; instead it creates a situation where children must work together in some fashion to complete their part of the task. Bonino and Cattelino draw attention to their observation that flexibility in thinking varies between girls and boys, with a stronger influence being recorded for boys. The issue of gender differences will be discussed later, but while most studies of collaborative problem solving form same-gender pairs, the influence of gender on the nature of the interaction and on any subsequent cognitive ability or learning is gaining increasing attention.

Blaye and Bonthoux (2001) examined the flexibility of three- to five-year-old children in relation to categorisation – in particular, their flexibility to re-categorise one object from one basis, such as taxonomically, to another, such as thematically. Most of the previous research, they claim, has looked at such flexibility between young children across different experimental conditions. Blaye and Bonthoux, in contrast, wished to examine under which conditions a child, any child, could shift categorical relations for a single object. They also took advantage of the spontaneous choices of the young children. Both taxonomic and thematic choices were elicited, in similar proportions, supporting the hypothesis that both types of relation are available to children as young as three years of age. These younger children, however, showed greater fluctuations in their choices, and these fluctuations were not consistent with the materials, unlike the categorisations used by older children. The research did demonstrate that categorical flexibility exists in young children and that it moves from 'spontaneous variability to adaptive flexibility' (Blaye & Bonthoux, 2001, p. 409), with consistency observed across the presentation of similar contextual cues. Why consistency of choice co-occurs with increasing adaptive flexibility is a research question that still needs answering, although Karmiloff-Smith's (1992) theory offers a possible solution. Consistency is interpreted as showing greater explicit representation of the underlying relationships between objects, and this may explain the developmental trend. So while cognitive flexibility has been shown to exist, to be measurable and something that shows a developmental trajectory, no-one has yet demonstrated how such flexibility may assist children when solving problems, particularly when they are working with another child.

Another way of conceptualising initial levels of thinking and how these may influence children's behaviour during collaborative problem solving is to look simply at cognitive variability (Zandt, 1999). The notion of cognitive variability derives from Piaget's theory, which characterises cognitive development by cycles of equilibrium and disequilibrium. The latter is an imbalance, where old levels of understanding are modified to take into account or accommodate new experiences. Learning best takes place when the organism – that is, the child – is in a state of cognitive disequilibrium. If this is the case, how can we identify the cognitive state of the child, and, if we can make this identification, how can it be used to benefit children's learning, particularly their collaborative problem solving?

Some answers to these questions are noted in the research conducted by Siegler and colleagues, who tried to identify behaviours that signal an impending change in learning or understanding. Variability in performance by children may indicate instability, which itself may be a marker of, or a prerequisite for, cognitive change. Alibali (1999) points out that, instead of looking for commonalities in children's thinking, perhaps variability should also be looked at as an explanatory mechanism for cognitive change. She also acknowledges that Siegler's work (discussed in Chapter 3) examines variability, particularly in strategy use, and that variability signals change, which could be important in the context of children's cognitive development and cognitive growth. Alibali's (1999) study examines the source of change, asking what causes children to develop or abandon particular strategies in problem solving and whether change is gradual or abrupt. In relation to the source of change, Alibali looked at children's initial level of variability, which is of central interest here, as well as the instructions given to the children – the external environment.

For the purposes of the current argument, children's initial variability was considered important because it should predict strategy changes made while solving problems. It was claimed that children with low levels of variability initially would generate strategies and increase in cognitive variability, while children with high levels of variability would abandon strategies and thereby decrease variability. It was further claimed that instruction as typically given in the school classroom, for example, would lead to strategy modification by children, and that different types of instruction may have different effects on initial variability and on strategy change. Alibali (1999) used a combination of gesture and speech to assess children's strategy use during problem solving to obtain a comprehensive picture of their strategic behaviour. The participants were nine-year-olds, who worked independently on paper-and-pencil mathematical problems. Gesture was included because of the contention that children, when solving problems and learning, often use gesture when explaining a new concept (e.g., Alibali & Goldin-Meadow, 1993; Goldin-Meadow, Alibali & Church, 1993). In particular, this same research notes that sometimes, when children's verbal explanations are less than adequate, their gestures suggest a fuller understanding. The 'gesture–speech mismatch' was also taken as indicative of an unstable cognitive system, perhaps in a state of readiness to change.

Alibali (1999) measured changes in variability by the children's explanation of the solution given at pre-test compared to the explanation given at post-test, examining the number of different strategies expressed. High variability was claimed throughout, with an average of around 2.5 strategies (both verbal and gestural) being expressed on both occasions. Some children increased in variability, while others decreased, although this did not depend on the instructions provided. Instructions did lead to variations in the patterns of learning and transfer recorded by Alibali (1999) but not, it is claimed, to any changes in the number of strategies available to the children. Contrary to expectations, pre-test variability was not related to whether new strategies were generated, but children with high initial variability did abandon strategies as predicted. Again, instruction played a role, with children generating correct and abandoning incorrect strategies after instruction. The quality of instruction varied but always included feedback along with some type of direct instruction. It was concluded that these forms of explicit instruction may in fact override any initial variability, since this was not linked to strategy generation. In general, however, this study did demonstrate that initial variability level has a role to play in the generation of strategies under some circumstances and to the abandonment of strategies when too many are available at the start. Alibali also notes that the changes could not be explained by a simple regression to the mean, as the abandonment of strategies was not paralleled by a generation of new strategies for children of different initial variability.

What this and other studies (e.g., Alibali & Goldin-Meadow, 1993; Perry, Church & Goldin-Meadow, 1988) have shown is that gesture can be as powerful as speech in revealing extent of knowledge in problem solving. Children who use gestures at a sophisticated level can benefit from instruction, which suggests that such gestures are a measure of early cognitive competence (Siegler & Stern, 1998) or an indicator of learning or strategy use at an unconscious nonverbal level before knowledge can be explicated at a conscious verbal level. This has implications for the study of collaborative problem solving, since the interaction between children takes places on both a nonverbal and a verbal level, and gestures might play a critical part in the establishment and maintenance of a working relationship that encourages learning.

Reynolds and Reeve (2002) examined the role of gesture in collaborative problem solving. The study aimed to investigate the extent to which gesture served as an amplifier for verbal communication, especially as a marker for shifts of attention on a problem solving task and as a means of elaborating meaning when the linguistic resources were inadequate. They also wished to see whether changes in speech tempo, including pauses, together with gestures, indicate change in conceptual understanding. Two female students were studied as they worked together in the classroom on problems related to the graphical representation of speed as a rate and of a bus journey. Protocols of two brief exchanges were examined for evidence of the co-construction of understanding.

In an intensive analysis of the verbal and gestural communication between the students, Reynolds and Reeve found that gestures were used during problem solving to establish and maintain joint attention on the problems. Gestures were also found to support the meaning of the language expressed by the students, and there appeared to be a relationship between gesture, speech speed and pauses and the propensity for cognitive change or learning. As this is one of the few studies to have examined collaborative problem solving, it is fascinating that it shows how gesture is related both to task and role regulation as well as to attentional and cognitive change. Gestures are an integral part of the communication pattern that leads to intersubjectivity as well as enhancing problem solving. The fact that gesture can contribute to our understanding of when children are ready to benefit from collaboration is important to a theoretical explanation of the usefulness of collaborative problem solving in facilitating cognitive change and development.

In a slightly different conceptualisation of how knowledge may change, Perry and Lewis (1999) investigated the role verbal imprecision ('humming and hawing') might play as an index of knowledge in transition. Verbal imprecision is characterised as containing restatements, comments on one's lack of knowledge and pauses – in other words, children become 'vague and inarticulate' (Perry & Lewis, 1999, p. 749) when their knowledge is unsure, unstable and changing. Using a physical causality problem solving paradigm, children worked individually but had to explain their solutions to the experimenter. These verbal explanations were analysed for verbal predictors of cognitive change. Furthermore, children received varying levels of instruction on the assumption that they were likely to benefit from instruction when in a state of transition. Children were aged between ten and twelve and a half years.

Verbal imprecision was coded from the verbal explanations provided in the pre-test so that learning outcomes could be predicted from the child's initial cognitive status. False starts, self-repairs, metacognitive comments, deletions (i.e., incomplete sentences) and long pauses were coded by two judges with an overall kappa of 0.83. Specificity of instruction ranged from a general manipulation instruction to a condition where full instruction was given in solving the problem. However, contrary to prediction, the instructional levels did not relate to eventual learning or improvement in problem solving.

All the measures of verbal imprecision were related to learning in so far as they predicted transitional knowledge; there were individual differences in the patterns of verbal expression reflecting different approaches to problem solution. Children were classified as full learners, partial learners or non-learners on the basis of the change in their performance from pre- to post-test. Full learners produced more false starts and self-repairs than the other types of learner, and this was interpreted as these children trying to reject old information (or ineffective solutions) while revising their approach. Metacognitive comments were statistically related to false starts and self-repairs and further related to the type of learning approach taken by the children who showed these types of verbal imprecision. Full learners also showed more long pauses, interpreted as being evidence for the children taking time to access a new approach and to make decisions about its use.

Perry and Lewis (1999) conclude that different types of verbal imprecision are linked with different types of learning and, in particular, knowledge change. They claim that the study elucidates how knowledge is organised for types of learning and problem solving and at different points in the learning process. It is now important that this research be extended to look at collaborative problem solving and whether verbal imprecision in one, other or both partners is in any way related to how children solve problems and how they learn. If verbal imprecision is an index of propensity to change or to benefit form instruction or collaboration, then research is needed to investigate this further.

Hosenfeld, van der Maas and van den Boom (1997) conducted a longitudinal study on the development of analogical reasoning in six- to seven-and-a-half-year-olds by examining five indicators of behavioural transition. They based their definition of transition on catastrophe theory, through which dynamic systems can be described and modelled. Transitions are viewed as abrupt changes, and the hypothesis tested by Hosenfeld et al. was that the development of analogical reasoning is discontinuous, reflecting a shift from unidimensional to multidimensional thinking. The five indicators of change are bimodality, inaccessibility, sudden jump, anomalous variance and critical slowing down. Each of these can be viewed as a type of assessable performance, which can be measured before, during and after working on the problems – in this case, analogical reasoning tasks – longitudinally. Changes in reasoning or thinking are marked by fluctuations in each of these indicators.

Eighty children participated in the study and were tested on analogical reasoning problems every three weeks for six months. Outcome data consisted of test scores, solution patterns and solution times. The catastrophe flags were identified in the order presented above as, should bimodality (accurate analogical reasoning versus inaccurate reasoning, based on free association) not be detected, then the discontinuity hypothesis is not supported. However, a large number of the children who initially used a free association solution switched to an analogy solution. This switch was accompanied by a 'sudden increase of analogy performance, a temporary increase of inconsistent solution behavior and a temporary slowing down of solution behavior' (Hosenfeld et al., 1997, p. 390). So the study showed that individual behaviours are indicators of cognitive change and could lend themselves to the study of problem solving, if suitable measures of performance and variability could be found.

Zandt (1999) attempted to address the perceived shortcomings in some of the previous research on cognitive variability. Noting that Hosenfeld et al. (1997) had taken problem solving time as an objective measure of variability and impending cognitive change, she investigated how initial individual variability in children was related to learning as manifested in pre- to post-test change. From Alibali's (1999) study, we know that variability does not always lead to cognitive change and that there are contextual factors influencing strategy generation and strategy abandonment, both indicators of change. However, it is still possible that some sort of cognitive variability is related to propensity or readiness to change. Zandt also studied the proposition that the way in which variability influences outcome may be through the behaviours, specifically the verbal behaviours, evidenced in social interaction.

Using a pre-test/collaboration/post-test design, Zandt (1999) studied 68 children aged around seven and nine years of age. Pairs were formed of same-gender, same-grade children, who worked on paper-and-pencil versions of the Orange Juice Task (OJT, a proportional reasoning task with increasing levels of difficulty), which enabled children to be classified on the basis of their cognitive ability, as well as permitting an analysis of any cognitive change. The pairs also comprised children of different ability as measured by pre-test performance. Performance measures were taken of level of ability (as established through correct responses on the task) and of variability, which was calculated on the basis of strategy use and solution times. Strategies were inferred from the performance of the children – based loosely on the characteristics of problem solving at the various levels identified for correct solution of increasingly difficult versions of the proportional reasoning task. Solution time was defined as the time from problem presentation to the final answer. For each level of the task, four problems were presented and solution time was averaged. The standard deviation of solution time across all levels was calculated for each child, giving a measure of individual performance, and classification was based on whether solution time increased from pre- to post-test by more than one standard deviation. The language used in collaboration was coded in accordance with the categories developed by Garton and Renshaw (1988) and examined interactive behaviours rather than individual behaviours.

Zandt (1999) found that both low and high ability children improved after social interaction, and that improvement was greatest for the older children. Differential improvements were noted depending on the initial performance level demonstrated in the pre-test. For both ages, less capable children showed greater pre- to post-test improvement than their more capable peers. In terms of solution time, there was no linear relationship between increasing problem difficulty and increases in time taken to solve the problems, while the number of strategies used was related to time taken. Younger children with more strategies took longer, while the converse was the case for older children – in other words, the number of strategies was negatively related to an increase in solution time.

Could pre- to post-test improvements be linked to initial cognitive variability (time taken and strategic variability)? In the case of the younger children, variability was a good predictor of improvement while, for the older children, the strength of the relationship was weaker but still positive. In particular, the use of a greater number of strategies at pre-test was associated with improvements at post-test for all children. The time factor was neither robust nor a consistent predictor of learning. Furthermore, an analysis of whether variability influenced the interaction behaviours showed that it was not linked to the provision of information or the extent to which the partners relied on each other during collaboration, with different relationships being demonstrated for increase in solution time and strategy use. Finally, Zandt (1999) showed that most of the interaction measures were not predictive of pre- to post-test improvements in any children, and only the number of disagreements during the interaction predicted learning.

So variability, as measured in this study by the number of strategies available for use at pre-test, predicted both pre- to post-test improvements on the proportional reasoning task and the use of an information provision style of collaboration during interaction. The more strategies the child had available, the greater the likelihood that the interaction would be characterised by agreements and, especially, disagreements between partners. Finally, through this route, the interaction predicted pre- to post-test learning. The role played by individual variablity (as defined and measured by Zandt, 1999) is relatively weak and probably indirect. This research highlights the potential role played by individual cognitive variability in determining learning in children but does not elucidate clearly either the direct or the indirect predictive capacity of such differences between children. Zandt herself points to shortcomings that may have limited the strength of her findings. Firstly, variability depends on the task, and certainly the proportional reasoning task lent itself to such measurement. The task has levels of increasing difficulty, the solution to which requires increasing cognitive abilities. Strategic variability across the different levels can be directly compared, which was not done here, so there is no across-level strategic comparison, only within level and only at pre-test. This is supported by the lack of evidence for the predictive utility of solution time, again only measured at pre-test, and hence there are insufficient data to make comparisons and stronger claims. Finally, although two measures of variability were included, they are not related as strongly, particularly in the older children, as may have been supposed from the work of Hosenfeld et al. (1997). They cannot therefore be taken as a single indicator of a child's level of understanding.

During the interaction, which of necessity is a social not an individual enterprise, children's variability was apparent through the language they used. However, unlike previous studies cited earlier, the instructional or information component of such an interaction would be neither as consistent nor as accurate as that provided by an adult such as a parent, experimenter or teacher. Such inconsistencies could well increase strategic variability and not necessarily in the positive direction!

FRIENDSHIP AND SOCIABILITY

There has been an ongoing debate in the collaborative problem solving literature about the value of pairing children who are friends. Friendship can be determined through, *inter alia*, asking teachers, asking the children to nominate their three best friends and sociogram analysis. It can be argued that friends are more likely to collaborate successfully since common knowledge, communication patterns and acceptable roles can be established quickly and often without much, if any, negotiation. Most collaborative problem solving research has, however, been conducted using pairs based on characteristics such as ability level and gender while ignoring friendships. Indeed, friends are often specifically excluded as problem solving pairs.

Much of the argument in favour of friendship pairs is summarised by Azmitia and Montgomery (1993) in their paper on the relationship between friendship and scientific reasoning. In particular, they explore whether collaboration between friends leads to greater cognitive improvements than collaboration between acquaintances. They also wanted to investigate whether the mechanisms involved in friendship mediate the development of scientific reasoning. Azmitia and Montgomery note that friendship interactions and conversations are marked by greater mutuality and involvement than those between non-friends, and that joint activity may be easier to establish, leading to enhanced social and individual learning. Nonetheless, they acknowledge that these characterisations of friendship have largely been studied in relation to children's social and emotional development rather than their cognitive development.

In their study, pairs of friends aged around 11 and a half years worked on an 'isolation of the variables' problem – a scientific reasoning problem that requires manipulation of a number of variables to obtain the correct answer. In addition, the problem can have varying levels of difficulty. Children worked in same-gender mutual friendship pairs, friendship being determined through peer nomination. Acquaintance pairs were formed of children who did not dislike one another. The study used a pre-test/ collaboration/post-test design, each one week apart, with 18 friendship pairs and 18 acquaintance pairs.

The interaction session was analysed using transactive dialogues with the assumption that friends would probably be more closely attuned to each other's justification of strategies and solutions. Transactive dialogues are defined as discussions in which the reasoning of each partner is dependent and relies on the reasoning of the other. Kruger's (1992) work informed the approach adopted in this study, as she had demonstrated the value of other-oriented transacts for subsequent moral judgements. Azmitia and Montgomery extended this work into the scientific reasoning domain and predicted that, because friends are able to monitor each other's reasoning more closely, their collaboration would result in greater cognitive improvements than the dialogues of acquaintances. The study investigated seven specific hypotheses based on this broad prediction.

The results focused on differences between friendship and acquaintances pairs' performance on the reasoning task, differences in dialogues and relationships between cognitive performance and quality/quantity of transactive dialogues. Azmitia and Montgomery (1993) found that friends demonstrated superior scores on the isolation of the variables task both during collaboration and independently at post-test, *but* the benefits were only recorded in the more difficult versions of the task. Friends, as predicted, checked and evaluated strategies and solutions and justified them spontaneously more frequently than acquaintances. The former produced more transacts, especially other-oriented transacts, and transactive conflicts were positively related to problem solving accuracy. Other forms of transacts, such as statements and questions, were not related to improved problem solving. Azmitia and Montgomery discuss the interpretations and implications of their findings but urge caution in claiming full support for their predictions. Firstly, the only type of transact associated with improved problem solving was conflict. They discount the explanation that there may have been a problem with their coding scheme, instead suggesting that adolescents' limited reasoning skill may itself have restricted the use of contiguous statements in non-conflictual dialogues. Any conflicts or contradictions may have led to a greater number of transactive discussions. They concede that as adolescents develop and grow older, they may become more capable of acting on and reacting to one another's dialogue, and that this may occur irrespective of whether the pairs are friends, acquaintances or strangers.

The second caveat is that friendships themselves have varying characteristics in terms of their intensity and endurance. In Azmitia and Montgomery's (1993) study, the adolescents had been friends for at least seven months, and the findings may not be applicable to more recent or less stable friendships. This observation is particularly pertinent when we consider young children and the role their friendships might play in assisting collaborative and subsequent independent problem solving. Young children's friendships are notoriously unstable, short-lived and fairly superficial, which means that any study of friends, acquaintances or other forms of pairings between young children may not be as straightforward as that of adolescent pairings, and any benefits that could be attributable to friendship may not be as clear.

In another study focusing on adolescents, Strough, Berg and Meegan (2001) examined how gender and friendship relate to differences in task interpretation and social problems that occur during collaboration in a classroom setting. A short-term longitudinal design was used, with the adolescents being studied over a six-week period while they worked on a Spanish project. Task and social demands were studied as they were both regarded as defining features of collaborative problem solving and are the elements usually manipulated in research studies. However, it remains unclear to what extent young people interpret or perceive these demands consistently with the researcher's intentions. So one of the aims of the research was to examine collaborators' interpretations of the collaboration, in the belief, bolstered by theoretical developments, that individuals' interpretations of task and social demands provide us with an under-standing of how they experience and approach tasks and social activities in everyday living. Social demands include those relating to roles and responsibilities or the division of labour, while task demands include man-aging, organising and designing the materials necessary for task comple-tion. Some people might regard one interpretation as more important than the other and might even interpret demands for either sort of problem dif-ferently. Strough et al. therefore manipulated the relative salience of task and social demands in relation to the gender and friendship composition of the pairs.

Drawing on the literature that considers children's friendships in general and gender differences in relation to social issues in particular, Strough et al. (2001) acknowledge the complexity of the areas and the paucity of research dealing directly with friendship and gender in relation to collab-orative problem solving in everyday contexts. In their study, they looked at peer groups who had self-selected, which enabled them to examine the children's own construction of collaboration based on the friendship and gender composition of the groups. They also studied whether interpreta-tions of problems were focused on the task or on the social demands of the collaboration, how the friendship and gender composition of the group related to the relative salience of the task and social demands, and how all these related to performance on the task.

Eighty-two adolescents with an average age of 13 and a half years par-ticipated in a collaborative project to meet class requirements. The project was to translate a skit from Spanish to English, memorise and practise the lines of the skit in Spanish, design props and costumes and present the skit to classmates. The 24 self-selected groups varied in size from two to six, and all but one were single gender. Friendship networks were obtained from peer nominations of the children's five closest friends, from which a network density score could be calculated. The salience of the task and social demands was assessed via children's ratings of the extent to which the items in a scale represented the sorts of problems they encountered. Items reflected both social demands (such as unequal distribution of labour) and task demands (the translation was hard; time is running out) and were completed independently, twice a week after group work. The actual week of the study varied so that any effect of the time of assess-ment could be minimised. Participants were each given an independent grade for the assignment, which was used as the performance measure.

As expected, the groups were formed on the basis of friendship and gender, and there were no gender differences in relation to levels of friend-ship or size of work group. The salience of the task and social problems identified by the children varied according to gender, friendship and time. In general, salience decreased over time, although, while task demands decreased in salience, social demands increased. Greater group friendship was related to less problem salience and less salience of social demands. Social problems were less salient to females than males. Gender, friendship and salience of social demands were related to final performance, with greater salience of social demands early in the study associated with better performance. Conversely, later salience of social problems was associated with poorer performance. Females generally outperformed males, while the benefits of greater friendship for males were noted in better performance.

Strough et al. (2001) discuss their findings in relation to the literature on friendships, gender, the relative influence of task and social demands on participants' interpretations of collaboration, and the benefits that accrue from different group compositions on performance in a classroom task over a six-week period. Social problems, relating to division of labour and so on, were less salient to females than to males, and, consistent with the literature on gender roles, males had a greater need to define and defend their role, tending to focus on dominance and self-assertion. Females, on the other hand, were more likely to use communication and co-operation to enhance agreement, consensus and collaboration, thus reducing the focus on social demands. In addition, greater friendship (as measured objectively) was associated with decreased overall salience of problems and less salience of task problems. This runs counter to the often cited reason for teachers not permitting friends, particularly male friends, to work together for fear they will disrupt one another. This research has shown this not to be so.

Again, the authors offer some shortcomings and reservations in relation to the findings. They acknowledge that there is some statistical interdependence between the individuals' interpretations as a consequence of their experience in the group. Group analyses yielded similar patterns to the individual results, even with reduced power due to smaller comparison groups. Statistical interdependence is a pervasive problem in the analysis of interaction and process data, and again provides an additional argument for the examination of individual differences in collaborative problem solving rather than looking at individual or group averages. Strough et al. (2001) recommend the use of both quantitative analyses of individuals and qualitative analyses of groups as a comprehensive way of dealing with all the data, while recognising the time-consuming nature of such an approach. A second limitation was the drawing of friends from within the classroom only, since these friendships may not extend to classes or situations outside that specific physical location. The subject,

Spanish, was an elective, and it was possible that friendship nominations were based on (perceived) competence and achievement of the other students. Even though achievement was not related to salience of task and social demands, it may be a relevant variable, especially if the course being studied was compulsory and not an elective. Therefore, both academic and social competence should be taken into account in collaborative problem solving.

The final limitation was that the data were of individuals' perceptions of task or social problems, not of the actual incidence of the problems. While there are advantages in using participants' own interpretations, they were assessed via an adult-developed instrument that may not accurately reflect adolescents' views. Solution of this dilemma is not immediately obvious, since even an interpretation taken from, say, videotapes of the interaction might also reflect an adult perspective. Maybe a combination of approaches is required here too. This paper, through its inclusion of a number of variables, allows for a wider range of theoretical perspectives to be considered in the study of problem solving in children. The main drawback of both this and the previous study (Azmitia & Montgomery, 1993) is that they were conducted with adolescents, whose friendship patterns, stability and durability may be quite different from those found in young children, who may not form homogenous groups, if the literature on friendship formation and development is correct.

Da Silva and Winnykamen (1998), in a study of six- to seven-year olds, examined the relationship between the sociability ratings of the children, their collaborative problem solving behaviour and their subsequent independent performance. Sociability was assessed by asking each child with whom they would play at recess or to whom they would talk. Children could nominate as many children, of either gender, as they liked. Each child then received a score based on the number of times he or she was nominated. Sociable children were those in the top third of the distribution, while not-so-sociable children were those in the bottom third. Problem solving ability was then assessed on two spatial tasks, which required the children to place shapes according to a model with some variations.

The hypotheses related to the children's degree of sociability and the types of collaborative problem solving. The literature on children's friendships and popularity draws attention to the greater capacity of popular children to demonstrate co-operative behaviours in social interaction, while children who are not so popular are isolated and act in a competitive and individualistic way. The general research question under investigation by Da Silva and Winnykamen (1998) was what happens when two sociable or two not-so-sociable children were paired when each of their individual skill levels were low or where one child had a high skill level and one had lower individual problem solving skill. Specifically, the researchers hypothesised that:

- in mixed ability dyads, collaborative problem solving between two sociable children would help the high ability child adapt his or her skills to those of the lower ability child, and that both children would benefit in terms of improved subsequent individual performance;
- in same ability dyads, sociable children would endeavour to work together to find a common solution, while not-so-sociable children would work more individualistically, with the sociable children benefiting most;
- in general, sociable children would display higher quality information during mixed ability interaction, since one child has the knowledge and skills, compared to same ability sociable dyads; and
- the nature of the information exchanged between not-so-sociable children would be of the same quality, regardless of dyad type.

Eighty children formed 20 sociable and 20 not-so-sociable dyads, with ten mixed ability and ten same ability pairings in each. The same ability pairs were all of children of low ability, and half of the same-sex dyads were girls and half boys. The behaviours (mainly verbal) exhibited during the interaction sessions were coded according to the research questions and included co-operative behaviours, such as attracting the attention of the other partner and asking questions, and individualistic behaviours, such as directive orders or injunctions. Two gaze behaviours were also coded. The data of interest are the measures of progress demonstrated by children of lower ability in pre- to post-test problem solving performance.

Da Silva and Winnykamen (1998) found that sociable children demonstrated greater improvement than not-so-sociable children, regardless of the type of dyad, while lower ability children in mixed ability dyads improved more than children who worked with same ability peers. Finally, there was an interaction between sociability and dyadic type, with sociable children demonstrating greater improvement after collaboration in a mixed ability dyad. It was argued that the verbal exchanges between sociable children allowed the less able child to improve. These exchanges were co-operative in so far as the children talked about solutions to the problems. And, as predicted, the not-so-sociable children displayed more individualistic behaviours. Da Silva and Winnykamen claim that their results support the position that popular, sociable children are able to relate more quickly and adapt to various social situations more easily than children who are not so sociable. Indeed, the creation of joint dialogue is a hallmark of sociability and, according to a Piagetian interpretation, underpins the ability to decentre, to become less egocentric and to take the perspective of the other person.

In a Vygotskian framework, the sociable children were interpreted as working together and co-operatively to solve the problems, unlike the less sociable children, who tended to work in parallel. This latter kind of problem solving does not lend itself to identifying discrepancy in skill level or, in other words, the zone of proximal development. However, the progress made by the less able children in same ability dyads was similar, regardless of sociability. So both the joint problem solving of sociable pairs and the individualistic behaviours of not-so-sociable children led to improvements. This was not the case for mixed ability dyads. It was concluded that 'social mediation takes place in different modes, depending on whether the children are sociable in their daily life' (De Silva & Winnykamen, 1998, p. 268). For sociable children, the dyad offered the opportunity for dialogue and communicative interchanges; not-so-sociable children, working individually, reorganised their thinking internally without recourse to their partner.

Rourke, Wozniak and Cassidy (1999) looked at partner sensitivity in peer conflicts among pre-school children. They acknowledge the extensive work that has been done on children's conflict behaviour and on the management of such conflict. They also note that young children display sensitivity to the type of partner with whom they are in conflict (e.g., parent versus brother/sister versus friend) but that there is a dearth of research into the degree to which such sensitivity varies within a relationship. Rourke et al. explored this issue by pairing children with others for free play. One group of children met with the same partner on four occasions, while another group met with the same partner for three sessions and a different one for the fourth. They compared the extent to which the behaviours in the first three sessions predicted those in the fourth. Behaviours included initiating conflict, duration of conflict episodes, the prevalence of conflict themes (object oriented/interpersonal) and the percentage of episodes solved/unresolved. Rourke et al. hypothesised that yielding (giving in/subordination) would be sensitive to the partner and therefore better predicted in session 4 in those children who remained with the same partner.

Rourke et al.'s work was consistent with earlier studies of preschoolers' conflict behaviours, which showed that conflicts were frequent, short-lived and solved by the children themselves, half being resolved by subordination. Furthermore, these conflict behaviours were sensitive to being with a particular partner. Children with the same partners throughout showed the same sorts of behaviours as those with different partners, but the main difference was that children who did not change partners yielded more in session 4 than the others. In general, the conflict behaviours were remarkably similar. Rourke et al. claim that these young children were showing quite sophisticated social awareness that overrides any individual factors (such as aggressive behaviour style) and that elements of the interactions with both the same and different partners support this. Their conflicts are characterised by a diverse range of behaviours, and the children are socially sensitive – that is, they have quite highly developed levels of social understanding and can respond differentially depending on the social situation and not just at the individual level. This study has therefore lent more support to the notion that interpersonal sensitivity is something possessed by, and measurable in, young children and that it can influence the outcome, be it conflict resolution or problem solving collaboratively.

O'Connor (2000) focused on what social factors may relate to the language used in collaborative problem solving and subsequent cognitive gain. Specifically, the social sensitivity of 52 nine-year-old children towards others was measured at pre-test, and the children were classified into three interpersonal sensitivity profiles: high, medium or low sensitivity towards others. Using a proportional reasoning task, children were also classified according to their cognitive performance at pre-test. The language used during the interaction was coded into the categories used by Garton and Pratt (2001). The results of this study confirm that less capable children who work with more capable partners are more likely to show pre- to post-test improvement than children working with partners of similar ability. Children who were classified as having high interpersonal sensitivity were found to be more likely to demonstrate improvement in their problem solving post-collaboration than children classified as having medium or low sensitivity. In addition, high sensitivity children were more likely to produce language that agreed with their partner and to exhibit problem solving gains. Medium sensitivity children also used more language that agreed with their partner compared to low sensitivity children, but did not demonstrate the subsequent cognitive improvement. These findings indicate that the relationship between interpersonal sensitivity, language use and subsequent improvement is complex and not linear. However, there is clearly a relationship between interpersonal sensitivity and language use in collaborative problem solving, and children who demonstrate greater social awareness benefit, either directly or indirectly, from such interactions, specifically through their use of language that agrees with their partner.

In a study conducted by Garton and Harvey (submitted), eight-year-old children were allocated to comparison problem solving pairs on the basis of their performance on a pre-test problem solving task and their social or interpersonal sensitivity classifications. Four groups of pairs were compared:

1. children with high reasoning ability and high interpersonal sensitivity were paired with children of low reasoning ability and high interpersonal sensitivity;
2. children with high reasoning ability and high interpersonal sensitivity were paired with children of low reasoning ability and low interpersonal sensitivity;
3. children with high reasoning ability and low interpersonal sensitivity were paired with children of low reasoning ability and high interpersonal sensitivity; and
4. children with high reasoning ability and low interpersonal sensitivity were paired with children of low reasoning ability and low interpersonal sensitivity.

This research examined the role of sociability as measured not through peer nomination but through responses to scenarios. The scenarios were developed to measure interpersonal sensitivity or empathy, which, it was hypothesised, may be linked to children's competence in relating to others and predisposition to the establishment and maintenance of joint communication and sharing (O'Connor, 2000). The questionnaire used scenarios to assess the extent to which children endorsed behaviours that were regarded as helping another child and showing awareness of the need to help others (Rogoff, 1998). The questionnaire was a paper-and-pencil task and used five different scenarios designed to represent situations at school familiar to the children. For each scenario, children were required to respond to a situation where they were to provide assistance to a peer in need within a school context. For example: 'One of your classmates is searching in the classroom for something he/she has lost. Your classmate tells you that he/she is looking for his/her library book. How important is it for you to help him/her find the library book?' Girls responded to scenarios involving female peers and boys were given identical stories with male peers.

A pre-test/collaboration/post-test design was used, with a paper-and-pencil problem solving task being presented on all occasions. In general, there was an improvement in problem solving performance on the post-test for children classified initially as low problem solving/high sensitivity, regardless of who they were paired with. In contrast, children classified as low problem solving/low sensitivity also demonstrated post-test improvement, but only when paired with high problem solving/high sensitivity children. As expected, children classified as high problem solving did not show significant improvements in their pre- to post-test levels, no matter who they were paired with. Pre-test behaviours were found to be predictive of post-test levels for children identified as having high problem solving abilities to start with, as was the problem solving level achieved in the collaboration.

The researchers concluded that social sensitivity does not have a direct effect but rather makes an indirect contribution to a child's capacity to acquire and/or use the skills required in the problem solving task. This conclusion is based on two findings:

1. Low ability children with high interpersonal sensitivity improved after interaction when they were paired with high ability children with either high or low interpersonal sensitivity. That is, high interpersonal sensitivity assists less able children to take advantage of interaction with a more capable peer and to show subsequent improved individual reasoning performance.
2. Low ability and low sensitivity children demonstrated post-test improvement after being paired with high ability and high sensitivity children. In this case, it appears that the interaction of the high sensitivity and the high ability assisted the lower ability children to improve after interaction. This conclusion is reinforced by the lack of improvement demonstrated by the lower ability children when paired with children of high ability but low sensitivity.

This pattern of findings suggests that social sensitivity can benefit children's learning in two pairings. Children with lesser ability but high social sensitivity are able to capitalise on the latter to take advantage of the learning opportunity afforded in the interaction with a more capable partner, no matter what their partner's level of sensitivity. Also, less capable children with lower levels of social sensitivity benefit from collaboration with children who are highly skilled and have higher levels of social sensitivity.

While more capable children did not demonstrate improvement in their problem solving levels from pre- to post-test after collaborating with less able peers, Garton and Harvey (submitted) note that their sensitivity and the sensitivity of their partner may have made an indirect contribution to post-test problem solving levels. In addition, their sensitivity and its effect on the lesser ability child appear to contribute to the final problem solving skill level of the lesser skilled child, rather than their own problem solving skill *per se*.

MOTIVATION TO COLLABORATE

In addition to factors such as individual skill levels, sociability and capacity to engage in interaction, there is the issue of motivation or wish to participate in collaborative problem solving. Gabriele and Montecinos (2001) discuss the role of motivational goals in the problem solving performance of lower ability nine- and ten-year-olds working with higher ability peers. This study starts from the premise that the processes involved in peer collaboration and the resultant cognitive benefits are poorly understood. In particular, in heterogenous groups, the gains are masked by the failure of some students to benefit. This has been interpreted as children in unstructured groups having different perceptions of the ability of others. Less able children expect high ability children to perform better, while the high ability children perceive themselves as having superior ability – hence a self-fulfilling prophecy for higher ability or higher status children, who stand to benefit most from interaction in unstructured groups. This leads to the study of status factors that may be influencing cognitive development in peer collaboration.

Gabriele and Montecinos (2001) highlight the theoretical reasons why achievement goals may be important in explaining how and why children engage in and learn from interaction with higher status (however defined) peers. They distinguish between learning goals, through which children try to understand their work and evaluate their performance against that of others, and performance goals, which are characterised, in children at least, by both inflated and poor performance relative to peers and by using social comparison and reference groups. In other words, children try to appear competent or incompetent and hence perform at levels that are incompatible with learning and benefiting from collaborative problem solving. The study then examined whether learning and performance goals influence low-achieving children's perceptions of partners' relative competence and their own participation and learning when working with higher-achieving partners during collaborative problem solving. Specifically, it was predicted that, if low-achieving children adopt learning goals rather than performance goals, they will benefit more from working with a high-achieving partner in terms of learning more and engaging in more active participation. It was also hypothesised that these low-achieving children would perceive their high-achieving partner as being closer in status to themselves.

Seventy children in grades 4 and 5 (children around ten years of age) participated in the study. Achievement was measured through scores obtained previously from a standard routine maths screening test, with low achievement status being represented by scores below the 40th national percentile rank and high achievement status represented by scores greater than the 80th percentile. In addition, a further inclusion hurdle requirement had to be met for students to be eligible for the study. Participants were paired with same-gender, same-grade children, 35 low-achieving children being paired with a high-achieving partner and then randomly assigned to a learning goal or performance goal condition. Boys and girls were equally represented in the pairings.

The goal manipulation instructions were inserted into the general instructions given to the pairs before they commenced work on mathematical word problems together and at certain points during the collaboration. One of the dependent measures – via a questionnaire – was the extent to which the manipulations led to students adopting learning and performance goals respectively. In addition, the learning of the pairs was assessed, as was the performance of the dyad (as opposed to the individual child) and the perceptions of the partner's competence. Verbal communication during the solution of the third problem was also coded using turn of talk as the unit of analysis, turns being separated by at least three seconds or being ended by a change of speaker. Each child was assigned a level of participation, with high level participation including statements that reflected planning, sharing answers and asking questions. Medium level participation was represented by unelaborated answers to questions, and simple acknowledgment of a partner's contribution and repetition.

Only data from low-achieving children were analysed, and it was first noted that only students who received learning goal instructions showed evidence of incorporating those into their learning. These low-achieving children showed better problem solving scores at individual post-test than children given performance goal instructions. No differences were found in the levels of verbal participation between children given the two different learning goal instructions, suggesting that motivational goals were not related to verbal engagement in the collaboration. It had been expected that low-achieving children motivated by learning goals would be more active participants in the joint problem solving with high-achieving partners, while those with performance goals would be more passive and accept their high-achieving partner's solutions readily. This was not the case, and Gabriele and Montecinos (2001) speculated that the performance goal instructions were not as successful in making the performance goals salient relative to the learning goals.

The failure of the results of this study to support a difference between levels of verbal participation corresponding to differences in learning outcome for low-achieving children given the two different motivational instructions suggested to Gabriele and Montecinos that verbal participation may be inadequate for explaining benefits in learning. What they propose instead is that low-achieving children, irrespective of the learning goal instruction, are able to capitalise on working with a more capable partner. The difference lies, they suggest, in how the help received from the high-achieving partner was used non-verbally by the low-achieving child. The proposal that the learner constructs how the goals are used in the collaboration receives some theoretical support, but this needs further study.

Of particular interest, as noted by Gabriele and Montecinos, is that the pairings were all of same-gender and same-grade children. This ensured that achievement status was relatively unconfounded. However, in classrooms this is not often achieved, nor is it necessarily desirable, as teachers assign students to work groups based on various characteristics to obtain different educational and social outcomes. Experimental studies are of necessity limited, and one thing that must be considered in studies of collaborative problem solving is how the manipulations translate into educational and classroom practice.

The studies described in this chapter have illustrated the need to take into account various 'input' features when studying children's collaborative problem solving. Individual differences in readiness to benefit, cognitive flexibility or variability, sociability, social sensitivity and motivation are as important as measurement of actual cognitive competence. Each or any of these factors, as well as friendship and gender, might play an important role in a child's capacity to work with a particular partner. Much of the early work on collaborative problem solving made implicit assumptions about the value of pairing friends or same-sex children, but there are perhaps more subtle aspects that need to be considered. Individual differences in psychological constructs, such as sociability or flexibility, may themselves be influential, but are more likely to interact with competence, gender and friendship to affect the nature of the interaction, which itself is then related to the outcome. The only thing that can be said with certainty is that collaborative problem solving is beneficial, particularly to children who enter with lesser competence. But, after considering a range of varied research, the relationship between the individual factors and the interaction factors and how they combine to affect the outcome cannot be stated with any confidence.

CHAPTER 6

SUMMARY, REVIEW AND IMPLICATIONS

The preceding chapters have explored theories of children's cognitive development through studies that consider the child as problem solver. In particular, attention has been drawn to children's problem solving when they are working, and learning, collaboratively and how social interaction influences the cognitive outcome. What can we infer from this overview, in terms of the implications for theories of cognitive development?

Chapter 2 reviewed two major existing theories of cognitive development, those of Piaget and Vygotsky, and how these have influenced, directly and indirectly, contemporary explanations of how children learn. Almost all explanations of children's cognitive development ultimately invoke Piaget or Vygotsky, and much of the research reviewed here involves a comparison between the two interpretations. Undeniably other theories exist, but most have limited application to collaborative problem solving. In other words, the study of social problem solving in children has inevitably limited the types of theories or approaches that have been influential. In general, with regard to social problem solving, the focus has been on the interaction itself or on the skills (i.e., existing relevant abilities) children bring to the interaction and to the task. This has resulted in studies that look, respectively, at conflict, co-operation and communication in interaction, or at the way children tackle the joint task based on their existing problem solving skills, including strategy deployment.

One area that I have not dealt with in this volume is the information processing approach to children's cognitive development. This is mainly because of the focus on children working together rather than on individual perceptual and cognitive processing of the particular materials used in the task. In information processing approaches, computational models are developed to account for how learning takes place and improves, and these are then applied to children's cognitive development. Some of the work by Siegler and colleagues, discussed in Chapter 3, takes this approach (e.g., Siegler & Shipley, 1995; Siegler & Shrager, 1984), as the models they developed aim to account for changes in children's strategy selection in specific learning situations. There is, however, a large body of work that has developed mathematical models of learning through proposing connections and networks, sometimes referred to as 'architectures', to describe increasingly sophisticated developmental processes. Such models are usually fairly abstract, if rich in detail, and deal with the basic mechanisms of cognitive development, such as perception or language. Also, they can usually only be applied within the domain they attempt to explain, such as lexical processing, for example. On the other hand, they can explain developmental stages and transitions as well as non-linear developments, such as where cognitive development abruptly spurts, or even regresses.

So while the major focus in the past has been on social problem solving and the role that interaction plays in supporting, encouraging and facilitating children's learning, more recent work has started to look at characteristics of individual children. Instead of looking at the cognitive processing capacities of the children, recent studies look at characteristics of children that may lead them to benefit from collaboration. Such characteristics include children's readiness to benefit from interaction, their cognitive flexibility, speed of problem solving, and even gender. In other words, rather than looking at ability *per se*, being able to capitalise on social interaction through awareness of a partner's competence or by adopting various roles in the interaction might be as helpful for children's learning as ability alone, if not more so.

Another trend in the literature has been the shift away from studying average performance of children and an acknowledgement that children's performance in problem solving on any task improves with age. There are, increasingly, descriptions of individual patterns of performance and how they may predict children's propensity to solve problems collaboratively and to learn. These patterns may include cognitive ability, strategy use, capacity to engage and work with a partner, and a willingness to learn. Some of these have been studied, either in isolation or together, and are allowing a picture to be drawn of children's cognitive development both in specific problem solving situations and in general.

WHAT AND HOW REVISITED

The questions asked at the start of this book related to both *what* develops and *how* it develops. In terms of *what* develops, the distinction between cognitive change, cognitive development and learning still remains. To some extent, these three represent terminological sloppiness, although efforts have been made to distinguish them. Furthermore, using these terms begs the question of the role of innate capacities. It would be easy to answer the question of what develops by recourse to innate or biological explanations, whereby cognitive skills unfold according to a predetermined timetable. This also answers the question of why cognitive development follows a progressively sophisticated route to adult capabilities. However, this view ignores the evidence that children demonstrate a variety of skills and knowledge across a range of domains. The research on children's developing cognition generally finds that major changes occur across domains: for example, when there is advancement in conservation, there is also advancement in analogical reasoning. Piaget's theory – along with its modern variants – is generally regarded as a domain-general theory, although there are certain limitations to his original theory that prevent it from being completely general.

Domain-specific theories of development have often been considered as innate in so far as what does develop is constrained by children's limited capacity to deal with the material (however defined) or the area of cognition being considered. These constraints are believed to be internal mechanisms, with both innate and learned components. Debate on the nature of these constraints and the ways in which they operate is extensive but not relevant here, as it is generally assumed, in accounts of social learning, that the object of theoretical and empirical interest is the role of the interaction. It would not be impossible to integrate domain-specific, partially innate explanations with social accounts of learning, but as the methodologies and the overarching conceptual frameworks are so radically different (notwithstanding the debates within each position), it would probably be imprudent to attempt to do so.

So, in looking at the *what* of cognitive development, this book has been guided by recent developments in collaborative problem solving and how this domain – if it can be called that, given its social nature – has been explored to enable advances in our theorising about children's development and learning and in providing plausible explanations. Goswami (1998), however, notes another distinction that can be made with regard to *what* develops – namely, the differentiation between qualitative change and quantitative change in cognition. Qualitative changes tend to be abrupt and involve new ways of thinking, whereas quantitative changes are slower. This distinction is mirrored in the two types of research discussed earlier – respectively, the changes in patterns of performance with age and the improvements in average performance with age. Although there is not perfect overlap between the research approach and the description of cognitive changes, qualitative change accounts often look at patterns of, say, strategy use in the solution of a particular problem, and how these vary with age. By contrast, quantitative change accounts measure specific abilities or problem solutions at certain ages and chart how the ability improves with age.

This distinction is further reflected in the terminology used. 'Cognitive change' refers to short-term development, often with known precursors. It is consistent with a qualitative approach to children's development, as short-term development can be abrupt and the precursors are generally described by a pattern of behaviours. 'Cognitive development' often refers to longer-term development with unknown precursors and is consistent with a quantitative approach, which focuses on average performance with scant regard to what ability and social factors lead to the performance. 'Cognitive development' is thus applied to improved performance across individuals, while 'cognitive change' takes individual performance, together with what affects that performance, into account. 'Learning', however, is applied to the description of cognitive change – that is, short-term measurable gain in performance in the individual child *but* usually without concern for the precursors. Typically learning is focused on the outcomes. Cognitive development as learning ignores these precursors, and, in any case, they are difficult to assess in the extended timeframe implied in development.

Cognitive change and cognitive development can therefore be distinguished and the distinction aligned with other theoretical considerations. Learning, however, it would seem, is applicable to both cognitive development *and* cognitive change. Additionally, learning can be regarded as but one part of 'obuchenie', a Russian word used by Vygotsky to describe the teaching/learning process (Garton, 1992). This implies a social component to learning, which, in child-centred accounts of development or change, is generally not acknowledged. By taking the social into consideration, and by looking at social interaction, the role of the other person in the child's learning can be studied. So, learning requires the involvement of another person and thus can be distinguished on these grounds from traditional cognitive development and cognitive change.

The focus on collaboration in particular, and social interaction more generally, allows for exploring the *how*. The term 'cognitive development' has been used in the title of the book because learning, I believe, does lead to long-term cognitive advances and, while the studies usually only look at cognitive change in the sense of short-term change, it is essential that a longer-term perspective is adopted. This has the benefit of looking at children, as they work with each other or with an adult, being facilitated, assisted or supported to grow cognitively and to consolidate knowledge.

How cognition develops has been described therefore as requiring a social component, as support and influence. Various studies have been described that demonstrate how peers and adults facilitate learning in children of different ages as they work on a range of problems. Consistent with trends identified by Siegler (1998) and described in Chapter 1, there is a focus on learning, and learning in collaboration. The nature of the interaction can both constrain and facilitate opportunities for learning, and research has moved away from attempting to describe how the social context encourages and supports learning to looking at what characteristics of the children can do likewise. This shift is seen in the move away from comparing average performance before interaction with average performance after interaction (also usually involving comparisons of children of different ages, using mixed model ANOVAs or MANOVAs) to comparing relevant patterns of behaviour before the interaction with both outcome measures, usually post-test performance, and performance during interaction or other features of the interaction itself. In other words, instead of studying the *how* by looking at change and what it is about the interaction that might influence that change, researchers have begun to relate directly aspects of children's existing behaviours to outcomes and, at this stage, speculate about how these might be affecting the interaction and hence influencing the outcome.

DIFFICULTIES YET TO BE SURMOUNTED

One of the major issues at this stage in the genesis of work in this area is that many of the studies have used different problem solving tasks. Most tasks share the common characteristics of having a goal or outcome that can be defined and measured, several means or strategies by which the goal can be achieved, perhaps some obstacles to immediate solution and sometimes other resources, such as a collaborative partner, that may assist. Manipulations of these variables have been noted throughout this book, mainly driven by the research question and the theoretical position adopted. All the problems described in this book have involved material that the child or children can handle or that requires written answers to problems presented visually, the so-called paper-and-pencil tests. Some of the means of presentation of the problems have been related to the children's age, while others relate directly to the type of problem solving under investigation.

Although I have tried to restrict the ages of children under consideration here to those who are likely to be in school and therefore will have had similar socialisation and cultural experiences, at least in an educational context, some of the illustrative studies have included primary school children and young adolescents. Given the variation in the tasks used and how they are represented, children's familiarity with the materials can vary enormously. This differential can, in turn, influence the nature of the interaction, especially the communication patterns that evolve. For abstract scientific reasoning tasks, children may not have the appropriate linguistic labels needed to discuss how to go about the task. On the other hand, tasks requiring coloured blocks or furniture to be sorted may require only a common language for colours, such as 'red' or 'blue', or for pieces of furniture, such as 'bed' or 'chair', which are readily available. Children can therefore launch into working out how they are going to work together, rather than trying to find a common vocabulary first. Furthermore, there may be differences between tasks that require manipulation of materials and those presented in a paper-and-pencil format. Some of these issues are the focus of current research efforts. In general, as noted previously, the problem is defined through the eyes of an adult experimenter, and whether the children perceive there to be problem is a moot point. Usually they are introduced to the materials as a 'game' that they need to work on together, and then some rules are given. There is frequently no suggestion that there is an achievable outcome or that the experimenter has some goal in mind.

Not only are there differences in the nature of the problems to be solved, but the type of collaboration also varies. Some of the work has been conducted with adults paired with children, and some with peer pairs. Usually, though, it is younger children who are paired with adults, usually parents and most often mothers, while older children are paired to work together, usually withdrawn from a school classroom or, occasionally, as part of the educational experience. Different forms of pairing are theoretically driven, or perhaps more accurately theoretically justified, but more frequently are paired through expediency. It is much easier to work with captive children in schools than to persuade mothers to bring their offspring into your lab on a university campus where parking is difficult and the venue, as a seat of higher learning, may be quite intimidating. Some of our work has tried to compare pre-school children, recruited through childcare centres, working with peers or with their mothers in identical circumstances on pre-school premises (Garton, Harvey & Pratt, submitted), but such direct comparisons are rare and difficult to organise.

A further difficulty, discussed in this book, is the measurement of what goes on in the interaction and how that relates to the effects of the interaction, if any. Much research has adopted the social influence approach, whereby aspects of the interaction are related to the child outcomes. Typically, research on collaboration examines the nature of the interaction for identifiable factors that may be regarded as beneficial for children's learning. Very often the focus is on the more adept partner's way of managing the interaction in terms of both actually solving the problem and dealing with the social roles. So really, the focus is not on the interaction but on the behaviour of the participants, including both verbal and nonverbal communication, frequently categorised to reflect the sorts of constructs that are advantageous to learning. In addition, these behaviours are regarded as supporting or facilitating the learning of the less expert partner in the collaboration.

As noted, recent research efforts have adopted a larger unit of analysis in social interaction – namely, the interaction itself instead of the individual. Learning can only occur through the interaction – when the collaboration constitutes the knowledge, shared jointly between participants. Any developmental change is qualitative, reflective of the collaboration and the roles the partners bring and adapt to the interaction. Individual growth and development can only be construed within a sociocultural framework that acknowledges the broader culture. In this way, the collaboration can be viewed as mediating the capabilities of the participants rather than simply supporting or encouraging those of the less able individual. Cognition is socially mediated, and the way the interaction acts as an intermediary is accorded central importance. Of necessity, the sorts of analysis that are conducted on the interaction itself are quite different from those that are concerned with individual changes in levels of expertise, skills and knowledge.

IMPLICATIONS

There are some major implications of the study of collaborative problem solving in children. There are educational implications, especially for what happens in the classroom. There are implications for the adult in the workforce, where there is an ever-increasing expectation that people will work in teams, on short- and long-term projects, and even in the virtual environments created by globalisation (both national in the case of Australia and international). And there are implications for developmental psychology theory. I will consider each of these in turn.

Educationally, the work on children collaborating on problem solving has practical applications for teachers in classrooms, particularly for pair and group work. How to pair children to maximise the benefits for both or all partners is something teachers need to know if they are using this strategy for teaching and learning. Clearly teachers cannot assess existing competencies or propensities for interaction or assess levels of cognitive ability every time they wish to encourage collaborative learning. They can, however, take into account issues such as the content of the material to be used in the collaborative learning exercise, the gender, age and friend-ship relationship of the children, and the extent to which verbal and non-verbal communication can be fostered or engendered in the interaction. In other words, teachers need to acknowledge the principles that research has shown to be relevant in collaborative learning, taking into account in general terms the factors that influence various pairings or groupings. Nonetheless, holding all these things in mind when dealing with a class-room of 30 five-year-olds may not be possible, but at least teachers should be shown the value of collaboration as a teaching/learning strategy, how to maximise the opportunities and which curriculum areas lend themselves better to joint interaction.

Interaction allows for active engagement with others, which has been linked to enhanced learning. This notion underpins current educational philosophy for changes to school structures and processes, such as the middle school movement. In addition, problem solving contexts have been demonstrated, at least with upper primary/lower secondary students, to foster such things as critical thinking and logical reasoning, as well as encouraging independent decision making and autonomy.

As far as broader implications for adults are concerned, it is becoming increasingly important that, as employees, we work in teams, whether it be for teaching at university, to provide administrative support to service industries or on particular projects. The need to be able to collaborate is emphasised in contemporary workplace practices, and advertisements for employment opportunities often state as essential 'the ability to work in a team'. Fellow workers talk about co-workers 'being a team player', and this is voiced as an advantage. Co-operation and collaboration are the cor-nerstones of team work, and having skills and expertise at defining roles and responsibilities, at negotiating or arriving at a shared understanding of a task, and designation of duties among and between team members are all essential to success. Success can be measured through the creation of a tangible outcome such as a report or a new design, by high colleague evaluations of performance and, of course, by monetary remuneration and promotion.

While team work is stressed in many work environments, this is usually face to face work, and decisions are made personally, through what are sometimes regarded as interminable meetings. Meetings are often the butt of jokes, but they are the forums during which planning, negotiation, and role and responsibility allocation take place, and shared decisions are reached about how goals are to be achieved. The structure of meetings is similar to collaborative problem solving. Translating these skills into virtual environments is a new challenge for a global economy where teams can be national and international. Videoconferencing has been with us for a while now, but real-time visual internet connections are more frequently being used. These forms of communication require different skills to establish and maintain a shared focus and to collaborate in the true sense of the word.

Finally, this exploration of the child as problem solver has enabled a discussion of a range of theories in developmental psychology and a stock-taking of where theories are heading in the twenty-first century. There is no doubt that there is a movement away from the study of the average child in isolation to the study of the child in a social and cultural context. With this move has come a need for different ways of looking at children's development, and the discipline is still trying to find alternatives to the study of children working one-to-one with an adult experimenter. Theories both inform and are informed by developments in experimental methods, designs and ways to analyse both qualitative and quantitative data. It is recognised that an adherence to a scientific methodology may have inadvertently limited the methods used in the study of children and, consequently, limited the ways in which theories are developed. The socio-cultural theories, with the unit of analysis being the interaction, itself a social construction of the minds of the participants, is offering a new way of looking at children's development.

In conclusion, the paradigm of the child as problem solver offers opportunities to evaluate different developmental theories and to conjecture as to how this paradigm can be used to underpin new methods in the study of children's cognitive development, and to perhaps lead to the development of new theories, or at least the extension of existing theories, of children's cognitive change, cognitive development and learning.

REFERENCES

Alibali, M.W. (1999). How children change their minds: Strategy change can be gradual or abrupt. *Developmental Psychology*, 35, 127–45

Alibali, M.W., & Goldin-Meadow, S. (1993). Gesture–speech mismatch and mechanisms of learning: What the hands reveal about a child's state of mind. *Cognitive Psychology*, 25, 468–523

Azmitia, M. (1988). Peer interaction and problem solving: When are two heads better than one? *Child Development*, 59, 87–96

Azmitia, M., & Montgomery, R. (1993). Friendship, transactive dialogues, and the development of scientific reasoning. *Social Development*, 2, 202–21

Bearison, D.J., & Dorval, B. (2002). *Collaborative cognition: Children negotiating ways of knowing.* Westport, CT: Ablex Publishing

Blaye, A., & Bonthoux, F. (2001). Thematic and taxonomic relations in preschoolers: The development of flexibility in categorisation choices. *British Journal of Developmental Psychology*, 19, 395–412

Bonino, S., & Cattelino, E. (1999). The relationship between cognitive abilities and social abilities in childhood: A research on flexibility in thinking and cooperation with peers. *International Journal of Behavioral Development*, 23, 19–36

Bronfenbrenner, U. (1979). *The ecology of human development.* Cambridge, MA: Harvard University Press

Bruner, J.S. (1983). *Child's talk: Learning to use language.* Oxford: Oxford University Press

Carey, S., & Spelke, E. (1994). Domain-specific knowledge and conceptual change. In L.A. Hirshfeld & S.A. Gelman (Eds), *Mapping the mind: Domain specificity in cognition and culture* (pp. 169–200). Cambridge: Cambridge University Press

Carpendale, J.I.M., & Lewis, C. (in press). Constructing an understanding of mind: The development of children's social understanding within social understanding. *Behavioral and Brain Sciences*

Case, R. (1985). *Intellectual development: A systematic reinterpretation.* New York: Academic Press

Case, R. (1992). *The mind's staircase: Exploring the conceptual underpinnings on children's thought and knowledge.* Hillsdale, NJ: Erlbaum

Castles, K., & Rogers, K. (1993). Rule-creating in a constructivist classroom community. *Childhood Education*, 70, 77–81

Chapman, M. (1991). The epistemic triangle: Operative and communicative components of cognitive development. In M. Chandler & M. Chapman (Eds), *Criteria for competence: Controversies in the conceptualisation and assessment of children's abilities* (pp. 209–28). Hillsdale, NJ: Erlbaum

Chen, A., & Siegler, R.S. (2000). Across the great divide: Bridging the gaps between understanding of toddlers' and older children's thinking. *Monographs of the Society for Research in Child Devleopment*, 65 (serial number 261)

Crowley, K., & Siegler, R.S. (1999). Explanation and generalization in young children's strategy learning. *Child Development*, 70, 304–16

Da Silva, E., & Winnykamen, F. (1998). Degree of sociability and interactive behaviours in dyadic situations of problem solving. *European Journal of Psychology of Education*, XII, 253–70

De Lisi, R., & Golbeck, S.L. (1999). Implications of Piagetian theory for peer learning. In A.M. O'Donnell & A. King (Eds), *Cognitive perspectives on peer learning* (pp. 3–37). Mahwah, NJ: Lawrence Erlbaum Associates

DeLoache, J.S., Miller, K.F., & Pierroutsakos, S.L. (1998). Reasoning and problem solving. In D. Kuhn & R.S. Siegler (Vol. Eds), W. Damon (Ed. In Chief), *Handbook of child psychology. Volume two: Cognition, perception and language* (5th edn, pp. 801–50). NY: John Wiley & Sons

Doise, W. (1978). *Groups and individuals: Explanations in social psychology.* Cambridge: Cambridge University Press

Doise, W., & Mugny, G. (1984). *The social development of the intellect.* Oxford: Pergamon Press

Donaldson, M. (1978). *Children's minds.* London: Fontana

Druyan, S. (2001). A comparison of four types of cognitive conflict and their effect on cognitive development. *International Journal of Behavioral Development*, 25, 226–36

Fawcett, L.M., & Garton, A.F. (submitted). The effect of peer collaboration on children's problem solving

Ferrari, M., & Sternberg, R.J. (1998). The development of mental abilities and styles. In D. Kuhn & R.S. Siegler (Vol. Eds), W. Damon (Ed. In Chief), *Handbook of child psychology. Volume two: Cognition, perception and language* (5th edn, pp. 899–946). NY: John Wiley & Sons

Flavell, J.H. (1979). Metacognition and cognitive monitoring. *American Psychologist*, 34, 906–11

Flavell, J.H. (1999). Cognitive development: Children's knowledge about the mind. *Annual Review of Psychology*, 50, 21–45

Flavell, J.H., & Miller, P.H. (1998). Social cognition. In D. Kuhn & R.S. Siegler (Vol. Eds), W. Damon (Ed. In Chief), *Handbook of child psychology. Volume two: Cognition, perception and language* (5th edn, pp. 851–98). NY: John Wiley & Sons

Fodor, J.A. (1983). *The modularity of mind.* Cambridge, MA: MIT Press

Freund, L.S. (1990). Maternal regulation of children's problem-solving behavior and its impact on children's performance. *Child Development*, 61, 113–26

Gabriele, A.J., & Montecinos, C. (2001). Collaborating with a skilled peer: The influence of achievement goals and perceptions of partners' competence on the participation and learning of low-achieving students. *The Journal of Experimental Education*, 69, 152–78

Garton, A.F. (1992). *Social interaction and the development of language and cognition*. Hove: LEA

Garton, A.F. (1993). Representation in problem solving. In C. Pratt & A.F. Garton (Eds), *Systems of representation in children: Development and use* (pp. 251–69). Chichester: Wiley

Garton, A.F. (2003). Cognitive development. In J.P. Keeves and R. Watanabe (Eds), *The Handbook on Educational Research in the Asian Pacific Region* (pp. 365–78). Dordrecht: Kluwer

Garton, A.F., & Harvey, R. (submitted). Social sensitivity as a predictor of the benefits of collaborative problem solving in children

Garton, A.F., Harvey, R., & Pratt, C. (submitted). The role of language during children's collaborative problem solving

Garton, A.F., & Pratt, C. (2001). Peer assistance in children's problem solving. *British Journal of Developmental Psychology*, 19, 307–18

Garton, A.F., & Renshaw, P.D. (1988). Linguistic processes in disagreements occurring in young children's dyadic problem solving. *British Journal of Developmental Psychology*, 6, 275–84

Gauvain, M. (2001a). Cultural tools, social interaction and the development of thinking. *Human Development*, 44, 126–43

Gauvain, M. (2001b). *The social context of cognitive development*. New York: Guilford Press

Gelman, R. (2000). Domain specificity and variability in cognitive development. *Child Development*, 71, 854–6

Gelman, R., & Williams, E.M. (1998). Enabling constraints for cognitive development and learning: Domain specificity and epigenesis. In D. Kuhn & R.S. Siegler (Vol. Eds), W. Damon (Ed. In Chief), *Handbook of child psychology. Volume two: Cognition, perception and language* (5th edn, pp. 575–630). NY: John Wiley & Sons

Goldin-Meadow, S., Alibali, M.W., & Church, R.B. (1993). Transitions in concept acquisition: Using the hand to read the mind. *Psychological Review*, 100, 279–97

Goodnow, J.J. (2001). Directions of change: Sociocultural approaches to cognitive development. *Human Development*, 44, 160–5

Gopnik, A., & Wellman, H.M. (1994). The theory theory. In L.A. Hirshfeld & S.A. Gelman (Eds), *Mapping the mind: Domain specificity in cognition and culture* (pp. 257–93). Cambridge: Cambridge University Press

Goswami, U. (1998). *Cognition in children*. Hove: Psychology Press

Hatano, G., & Wertsch, J.V. (2001). Sociocultural approaches to cognitive development: The constituents of culture in the mind. *Human Development*, 44, 77–83

Hogan, D.M., & Tudge, J.R.H. (1999). Implications of Vygotsky's theory for peer learning. In A.M. O'Donnell & A. King (Eds), *Cognitive perspectives on peer learning* (pp. 39–65). Mahwah, NJ: Lawrence Erlbaum Associates

Hosenfeld, B., van der Maas, H.L.J., & van den Boom, D.C. (1997). Indicators of discontinuous change in the development of analogical reasoning. *Journal of Experimental Child Psychology*, 64, 367–95

Kail, R. (1979). *The development of memory in children.* San Francisco: W.H. Freeman

Karmiloff-Smith, A. (1992). *Beyond modularity: A developmental perspective on cognitive science.* Cambridge, MA: MIT Press

King, A. (2002). Structuring peer interaction to promote high-level cognitive processing. *Theory into Practice*, 41, 33–9

Kruger, A.C. (1992). The effect of peer and adult–child transactive discussions on moral reasoning. *Merrill-Palmer Quarterly*, 38, 191–211

Kruger, A.C. (1993). Peer collaboration, conflict, cooperation, or both? *Social Development*, 2, 165–82

Kruger, A.C., & Tomasello, M. (1986). Transactive discussions with peers and adults. *Developmental Psychology*, 22, 681–5

Kuhn, D. (1998). Afterword to Volume 2: Cognition, perception and language. In D. Kuhn & R.S. Siegler (Vol. Eds), W. Damon (Ed. In Chief), *Handbook of child psychology. Volume two: Cognition, perception and language* (5th edn, pp. 979–81). NY: John Wiley & Sons

Kuhn, D. (2001). How do people know? *Psychological Science*, 12, 1–8

Kuhn, D., Garcia-Mila, M., Zohar, A., & Andersen, C. (1995). Strategies of knowledge acquisition. *Monographs of the Society for Research in Child Development*, 60 (serial number 245)

Lerner, R.M. (1998). Theories of human development: Contemporary perspectives. In R.M. Lerner (Vol. Ed.), W. Damon (Ed. In Chief), *Handbook of child psychology. Volume one: Theoretical models of human development* (5th edn, pp. 1–24). NY: John Wiley & Sons

Levin, I., & Druyan, S. (1993). When sociocognitive transaction among peers fails: The case of misconceptions in science. *Child Development*, 64, 1571–91

Nelson-Le Gall, S.A. (1985). Necessary and unnecessary help seeking in children. *Journal of Genetic Psychology*, 148, 53–62

Nelson-Le Gall, S.A., DeCooke, P., & Jones, E. (1989). Children's self-perceptions of competence and help seeking. *Journal of Genetic Psychology*, 150, 457–9

Nelson-Le Gall, S.A., Kratzer, L., Jones, E., & DeCooke, P. (1990). Children's self-assessment of performance and task-related help seeking. *Journal of Experimental Child Psychology*, 49, 245–63

O'Connor, J. (2000). The relationship between interpersonal sensitivity and language use in children's collaborative problem solving. Unpublished BA Honours thesis, University of Melbourne

O'Donnell, A.M., & King, A. (Eds) (1999). *Cognitive perspectives on peer learning.* Mahwah, NJ: Lawrence Erlbaum Associates

Palincsar, A.S., & Herrenkohl, L.R. (2002). Designing collaborative learning contexts. *Theory into Practice*, 41, 26–32

Perret-Clermont, A.-N. (1980). *Social interaction and cognitive development in children.* London: Academic Press

Perry, M., Church, R.B., & Goldin-Meadow, S. (1988). Transitional knowledge in the acquisition of concepts. *Cognitive Development*, 3, 359–400

Perry, M., & Lewis, J.L. (1999). Verbal imprecision as an index of knowledge in transition. *Developmental Psychology*, 35, 749–59

Piaget, J. (1932). *The moral judgment of the child*. London: Routledge and Kegan Paul

Puustinen, M. (1998). Help-seeking behaviour in a problem-solving situation: Development of self-regulation. *European Journal of Psychology of Education*, XIII, 271–82

Radziszewska, B., & Rogoff, B. (1991). Children's guided participation in planning imaginary errands with skilled adult or peer partners. *Developmental Psychology*, 27, 381–9

Reeve, R.A., Garton, A.F., & O'Connor, J. (2002). The role of interpersonal sensitivity in collaborative problem solving interactions. Poster presented at the 17th Biennial meetings of ISSBD, Ottawa, Canada

Reynolds, F.J., & Reeve, R.A. (2002). Gesture in collaborative mathematics problem-solving. *Journal of Mathematical Behavior*, 20, 447–60

Rogoff, B. (1990). *Apprenticeship in thinking: Cognitive development in social context*. New York: Oxford University Press

Rogoff, B. (1998). Cognition as a collaborative process. In D. Kuhn & R.S. Siegler (Vol. Eds), W. Damon (Ed. In Chief), *Handbook of child psychology. Volume two: Cognition, perception and language* (5th edn, pp. 679–744). NY: John Wiley & Sons

Rourke, M.T., Wozniak, R.H., & Cassidy K.W. (1999). The social sensitivity of preschoolers in peer conflicts: Do children act differently with different peers? *Early Education and Development*, 10, 209–27

Shrager, J., & Siegler, R.S. (1998). SCADS: A model of children's strategy choices and strategy discoveries. *Psychological Science*, 9, 405–10

Shweder, R.A., Goodnow, J.J., Hatano, G., Levine, R.A., Markus, H., & Miller, P. (1998). The cultural psychology of development: One mind, many modalities. In R.M. Lerner (Vol. Ed.), W. Damon (Ed. In Chief), *Handbook of child psychology. Volume one: Theoretical models of human development* (5th edn, pp. 865–937). NY: John Wiley & Sons

Siegler, R.S. (1976). Three aspects of cognitive development. *Cognitive Psychology*, 8, 481–520

Siegler, R.S. (1981). Developmental sequences within and between concepts. *Monographs of the Society for Research in Child Development*, 46 (serial number 189)

Siegler, R.S. (1995). How does change occur: A microgenetic study of number conservation. *Cognitive Psychology*, 25, 225–73

Siegler, R.S. (1996). *Emerging minds: The process of change in children's thinking*. New York: Oxford University Press

Siegler, R.S. (1998). Forward to Volume 2: Cognition, Perception and Language. In D. Kuhn & R.S. Siegler (Vol. Eds), W. Damon (Ed. In Chief), *Handbook of child psychology. Volume two: Cognition, perception and language* (5th edn, pp. xxi–xxiv). NY: John Wiley & Sons

Siegler, R.S. (2000). The rebirth of children's learning. *Child Development*, 71, 26–35

Siegler, R.S., & Jenkins, E. (1989). *How children discover new strategies*. Hillsdale, NJ: Erlbaum

Siegler, R.S., & Lemaire, P. (1997). Older and younger adults' strategy choices in multiplication: Testing predictions of ASCM via the choice/no choice method. *Journal of Experimental Psychology: General*, 126, 71–92

Siegler, R.S., & Shipley, C. (1995). Variation, selection and cognitive change. In T. Simon & G. Halford (Eds), *Developing cognitive competence: New approaches to process modeling* (pp. 31–76). Hillsdale, NJ: Erlbaum

Siegler, R.S., & Shrager, J. (1984). Strategy choices in addition and subtraction: How do children know what to do? In C. Sophian (Ed.), *Origins of cognitive skills* (pp. 229–93). Hillsdale, NJ: Erlbaum

Siegler, R.S., & Stern, E. (1998). A microgenetic analysis of conscious and unconscious strategy discoveries. *Journal of Experimental Psychology: General*, 127, 377–97

Strough, J., Berg, C.A., & Meegan, S.P. (2001). Friendship and gender differences in task and social interpretations of peer collaborative problem solving. *Social Development*, 10, 1–22

Teasley, S.D. (1995). The role of talk in children's peer collaborations. *Developmental Psychology*, 31, 207–20

Thelen, E. (2000). Motor development as foundation and future of developmental psychology. *International Journal of Behavioral Development*, 24, 385–97

Thelen, E., & Smith, L.B. (1994). *A dynamic systems approach to the development of cognition and action*. Cambridge, MA: MIT Press

Thornton, S. (1995). *Children solving problems*. Cambridge, MA: Harvard University Press

Thornton, S. (1999). Creating the conditions for cognitive change: The interaction between task structures and specific strategies. *Child Development*, 70, 588–603

Tryphon, A., & Vonèche, J. (Eds) (1996). *Piaget – Vygotsky: The social genesis of thought*. Hove: Psychology Press

Tudge, J.R.H. (1992). Processes and consequences of peer collaboration: A Vygotskian analysis. *Child Development*, 63, 1364–79

Tudge, J.R.H., & Rogoff, B. (1989). Peer influences on cognitive development: Piagetian and Vygotskian perspectives. In M. Bornstein & J.S. Bruner (Eds), *Interaction in human development* (pp. 17–40). Hillsdale, NJ: LEA

Tudge, J.R.H., & Winterhoff, P. (1993). Can young children benefit from collaborative problem solving? Tracing the effects of partner competence and feedback. *Social Development*, 2, 242–59

Tudge, J.R.H., Winterhoff, P.A., & Hogan, D.M. (1996). The cognitive consequences of collaborative problem solving with and without feedback. *Child Development*, 67, 2892–909

Valsiner, J. (1998). The development of the concept of development: Historical and epistemological perspectives. In R.M. Lerner (Vol. Ed.), W. Damon (Ed. In Chief), *Handbook of child psychology. Volume one: Theoretical models of human development* (5th edn, pp. 189–232). NY: John Wiley & Sons

Van Meter, P., & Stevens, R.J. (2000). The role of theory in the study of peer collaboration. *The Journal of Experimental Education*, 69, 113–27

Vygotsky, L. (1978). *Mind in society: The development of higher mental processes.* Cambridge, MA: Harvard University Press

Vygotsky, L. (1986). *Thought and language.* Cambridge, MA: MIT Press

Webb, N.M. (1989). Peer interaction and learning in small groups. *International Journal of Educational Research*, 13, 21–39

Webb, N.M., & Favier, S. (1999). Developing productive group interaction in middle school mathematics. In A.M. O'Donnell & A. King (Eds), *Cognitive perspectives on peer learning* (pp. 117–49). Mahwah, NJ: Lawrence Erlbaum Associates

Wellman, H.M. (1990). *The child's theory of mind.* Cambridge, MA: MIT Press

Wellman, H., & Gelman, S. (1998). Knowledge acquisition in foundational domains. In D. Kuhn & R.S. Siegler (Vol. Eds), W. Damon (Ed. In Chief), *Handbook of child psychology. Volume two: Cognition, perception and language* (5th edn, pp. 523–74). NY: John Wiley & Sons

Wertsch, J.V. (Ed.) (1985). *Culture, communication and cognition.* Cambridge: Cambridge University Press

Wertsch, J.V., McNamee, G.D., McLane, J.B., & Budwig, N.A. (1980). The adult–child dyad as a problem-solving system. *Child Development*, 51, 1215–21

Wood, D., Bruner, J.S., & Ross, G. (1976). The role of tutoring in problem solving. *Journal of Child Psychology and Psychiatry*, 17, 89–100

Woodward, A.L., & Markman, E.M. (1998). Early word learning. In D. Kuhn & R.S. Siegler (Vol. Eds), W. Damon (Ed. In Chief), *Handbook of child psychology. Volume two: Cognition, perception and language* (5th edn, pp. 371–420). NY: John Wiley & Sons

Wozniak, R.H. (1996). Qu'est-ce que l'intelligence? Piaget, Vygotsky and the 1920 crisis in psychology. In A. Tryphon & J. Vonèche (Eds), *Piaget – Vygotsky: The social genesis of thought* (pp. 11–24). Hove: Psychology Press

Zandt, F. (1999). Effect of initial variability in problem solving on children's collaborative learning. Unpublished BA Honours thesis, University of Melbourne.

AUTHOR INDEX

SUBJECT INDEX